The Ps

Mana

Building and Sustaining a Strong Organizational Structure and Culture

The Psychology of Management

Building and Sustaining a Strong Organizational Structure and Culture

Sanchit Khullar

The Readers Paradise
New Delhi - 110002

The Psychology of Management

Sanchit Khullar

ISBN - 978-93-5977-278-3

Published by The Readers Paradise
www.thereadersparadise.com

Printed and bound by CPI Group (UK) Ltd, Croydon, CR0 4YY
Printed in UK

Cover Design by Kamini Bijoria

Typeset by The Readers Paradise

First Edition: 2024

FSC
www.fsc.org
MIX
Paper | Supporting responsible forestry
FSC® C171272

Preface

The way people think, feel, and interact with one another has always been a powerful determinant of success in any professional environment. Yet, until recent decades, the "soft" elements of human psychology were often overshadowed by more technical or strategic considerations in the realm of management. In today's complex and fast-paced world, however, effective management cannot afford to overlook the vital role that psychology plays in shaping productive, engaged, and resilient organizations. This book, *The Psychology of Management*, aims to provide readers with a foundational understanding of the psychological principles that drive effective management and foster a healthier, more dynamic workplace.

This work is divided into four main parts, each addressing a critical area where psychology intersects with management practices. In ***Part I: Foundations of Management Psychology***, readers are introduced to the essential psychological concepts that underlie workplace behavior, offering insights into human behavior and personality that serve as a base for all management practices. Here, we explore key personality theories and delve into how tools like the Myers-Briggs Type Indicator (MBTI) and Big Five Personality Traits can enhance leadership effectiveness and decision-making processes in real-world settings.

Moving forward, ***Part II: Psychological Approaches to Management*** delves deeper into cognitive processes and decision-making, showing how psychological insights can guide managers through the mental hurdles they face daily. This section unpacks the psychological traits of successful leaders and examines the indispensable role of emotional intelligence in leadership. It also discusses motivation and engagement, equipping managers with strategies to drive their teams' enthusiasm and productivity while nurturing their growth and development.

In ***Part III: Organizational Behavior and Culture***, the focus shifts to the psychological underpinnings of communication, team dynamics, and organizational culture. This section examines the psychological barriers to effective communication and explores how managers can resolve conflicts and build strong, professional relationships. It also delves into the psychological complexities of team dynamics and organizational culture, emphasizing the importance of creating a cohesive yet adaptable workplace culture that encourages both individual and collective success.

The final section, ***Part IV: Applying Psychology to Management Practices***, provides practical applications of psychological principles, guiding readers in performance management, stress reduction, and fostering innovation. Managers will gain insights into managing workplace stress and promoting well-being, as well as strategies for sparking creativity and guiding innovative thinking. The book concludes with a look at future trends and challenges, helping managers anticipate and prepare for the psychological impacts of evolving work models, technological advancements, and shifting workplace paradigms.

Each chapter is designed not only to present psychological theories and concepts but also to bridge them with actionable management strategies, enriched with case studies and practical exercises. Readers will find tools to assess and develop their own leadership skills and understand the psychological dynamics of their teams and organizations, empowering them to lead with both confidence and compassion.

The journey through ***The Psychology of Management*** is not merely academic; it's a practical exploration into becoming a more insightful, adaptive, and effective manager in today's world. By the end of this book, readers will possess a toolkit that blends psychological knowledge with management acumen, paving the way for organizations that don't just succeed, but thrive.

Author

Contents

Introduction

Welcome to "The Psychology of Management," a book designed to bridge the gap between the nuanced realms of psychology and the dynamic world of management. This guide is tailored for managers, leaders, and corporate professionals across the United Kingdom who are keen to refine their leadership skills through a deeper understanding of psychological principles. Whether you are a seasoned executive or a nascent manager stepping into the arena of corporate leadership, this book offers insights that will enhance your managerial acumen and interpersonal dynamics within the workplace. Management, in its essence, is about people. As such, understanding the psychological underpinnings of human behaviour becomes a critical tool for any effective manager. From decision-making and leadership to motivation and team dynamics, the psychological elements inherent in these areas are vast and varied. "The Psychology of Management" delves into these aspects, offering a comprehensive look at how psychological theories and practices can be applied to real-world management scenarios. The structure of this book is designed to guide you through the foundational theories of psychology as they apply to management, before advancing to more complex applications and contemporary challenges. It begins with an exploration of basic psychological concepts—such as motivation, perception, and learning—and how these influence everyday management tasks. We then move into leadership psychology, discussing the traits of effective leaders and the impact of various leadership styles on organisational culture and employee well-being. A significant portion of this guide is dedicated to practical applications. Here, you will learn about effective communication strategies, methods for enhancing employee motivation and engagement, and techniques for managing diverse and cross-functional teams. Additionally, the book addresses the psychological aspects of organisational change—a topic of paramount importance in today's rapidly evolving business environment. This book also recognises the increasing complexity of the modern workplace. Topics such as the psychology of remote work, the impact of technology on management practices, and the importance of mental health in the workplace are explored in depth. These sections are particularly relevant as businesses adapt to new ways of working and as managers are required to navigate through these transformations effectively. Throughout "The Psychology of Management," you will find a range of real-life examples, case studies, and anecdotes from successful UK-based companies. These are not only illustrative but also provide contextual insights that can be mirrored or adapted to your specific managerial contexts. Moreover, each chapter concludes with a set of actionable strategies, ensuring that the insights gained can be directly applied to your organisational and leadership challenges. As we embark on this journey together, it is my hope that this book will serve not just as a manual for current managers but also as a foundational pillar for those who aspire to lead. Management is an art refined by science, and by integrating psychological principles into your management style, you are setting the stage for enhanced effectiveness and success. Thank you for choosing to explore the fascinating intersection of psychology and management. May the knowledge you gain here inspire and equip you to lead with wisdom, empathy, and foresight.

Part–I

Foundations of Management Psychology

Chapter–1

Understanding Human Behavior

"The greatest discovery of my generation is that human beings can alter their lives by altering their attitudes of mind." – William James

Understanding human behavior is essential for effective management, as it forms the foundation of organizational dynamics. Basic psychological concepts such as motivation, perception, and learning play a pivotal role in shaping workplace behavior. Motivation drives employees to achieve their goals, impacting productivity and job satisfaction. Perception influences how individuals interpret their work environment, affecting their attitudes and interactions. Learning fosters adaptability and innovation, crucial for meeting the changing demands of the workplace.

Basic Psychological Concepts

1. Motivation

- **Definition and Importance**: Motivation is the internal engine that drives individuals toward achieving specific objectives. In the context of the workplace, understanding what motivates employees is essential for boosting productivity and enhancing job satisfaction.

- **Theoretical Frameworks**:
  - **Maslow's Hierarchy of Needs**: This theory suggests that individuals seek to satisfy a series of needs from the most basic, such as physiological and safety needs, to higher-level needs like esteem and self-actualization.
  - **Self-Efficacy**: As proposed by Albert Bandura, self-efficacy is crucial in motivation, representing the belief in one's capability to achieve a task. "People who regard themselves as highly efficacious act, think, and feel differently from those who perceive themselves as inefficacious. They produce their own future, rather than simply foretell it," Bandura noted.

2. Perception

- **Role in Management**: Perception involves the interpretation of sensory information to represent and understand the environment. In a managerial context, leaders' perceptions of team members and organizational actions significantly affect workplace dynamics.
- **Perception and Decision Making**: Managers' perceptions influence their decisions on delegation, promotions, and evaluations. Employee perceptions of management actions also impact their engagement and productivity.
- **Perceptual Biases**: Recognizing biases like the 'halo effect', where one positive attribute of a person

overshadows other aspects of their performance, is crucial for managerial fairness.

3. Learning

- **Continuous Development**: Learning in the workplace is about acquiring and applying knowledge and skills in response to changing job demands and technological advancements.
- **Learning Theories**:
  - **Experiential Learning**: David Kolb's theory emphasizes that learning is a process where knowledge arises through the transformation of experience. This model advocates for a cycle of learning that includes concrete experience, reflective observation, abstract conceptualization, and active experimentation.
- **Organizational Learning**: An organization that learns is one that adapts continually to an ever-changing environment. This is vital for maintaining competitiveness and fostering innovation.

Influence on Workplace Behavior

The interaction of motivation, perception, and learning within an organization informs a multitude of workplace behaviors.

1. Motivation and Employee Engagement

- **Proactivity and Initiative**: Motivated employees are more likely to take initiative and demonstrate commitment to organizational goals. "To win in the marketplace you must first win in the workplace,"

Doug Conant, former CEO of Campbell's Soup, famously said, highlighting the direct link between employee motivation and organizational success.

- **Retention and Turnover**: A well-motivated workforce is characterized by lower turnover rates, which translates into cost savings on recruitment and training for the company.

2. Perception and Organizational Climate

- **Impact of Managerial Actions**: How employees perceive the actions of their managers—from communication to decision-making—can significantly influence their job satisfaction and performance.
- **Creating a Positive Perception**: Managers need to be transparent and consistent to foster a positive perception, which can enhance trust and loyalty within the team.

3. Learning and Adaptability

- **Skill Development and Innovation**: Continuous learning environments enable employees to acquire new skills and refine existing ones, fostering a culture of innovation and problem-solving.
- **Learning from Failures**: Encouraging a mindset where failures are seen as learning opportunities can lead to significant improvements in performance. As John Maxwell puts it, "Fail early, fail often, but always fail forward," suggesting that the act of failing is not to be shunned but embraced as a powerful source of growth and innovation.

Chapter–2

Personality and Management

"The meeting of two personalities is like the contact of two chemical substances: if there is any reaction, both are transformed." – Carl Jung

Understanding personality and its significance in management is crucial for fostering effective leadership and team dynamics. Key personality traits theories provide valuable insights into the various dimensions of individual differences, enabling managers to comprehend and leverage the unique characteristics of their team members. Additionally, personality assessment tools play a vital role in talent management and leadership strategies, offering a means to gauge individual traits, preferences, and potential

Overview of Key Personality Theories

1. Trait Theory

- **Definition**: Trait theory posits that personality is composed of a number of traits, which are consistent patterns of thoughts, feelings, and behaviors that differ among individuals.
- **Relevance to Management**: Understanding the

traits of employees can help managers predict behaviors in various situations, such as stress or teamwork, enhancing the alignment of roles and responsibilities to individual capabilities.

2. **Psychodynamic Theory**
   - **Foundation**: Developed by Sigmund Freud, this theory emphasizes the influence of the unconscious mind on behavior, suggesting that human behavior is the result of desires, impulses, and memories that lie beyond conscious awareness.
   - **Management Implications**: This theory can help managers understand deeper underlying factors that influence employee behaviors, particularly in conflict resolution and motivational strategies.

3. **Humanistic Theory**
   - **Core Idea**: This approach views people as inherently good and focuses on the individual's potential for growth.
   - **Application in the Workplace**: Encourages supportive management practices that aim to develop the potential of employees, fostering an environment where individuals feel valued and are encouraged to fulfill their potential.

Personality Assessment Tools and Their Relevance to Management

1. **Myers-Briggs Type Indicator (MBTI)**
   - **Utility**: Helps determine the personality type of employees, which can guide team composition and leadership approaches.

- **Management Application**: By understanding whether an employee is an introvert or extrovert, a thinker or a feeler, managers can tailor their communication and leadership styles to suit individual employee needs.

2. The Big Five Personality Traits

- **Components**: Openness, Conscientiousness, Extraversion, Agreeableness, and Neuroticism.
- **Use in Management**: This model is particularly useful in recruitment and selection processes, helping predict how well candidates will fit the job and the organizational culture.

3. 360-Degree Feedback

- **Description**: Involves collecting feedback about an individual from their work circle, including peers, subordinates, and supervisors.
- **Significance**: Provides a comprehensive view of an individual's interpersonal, leadership, and management skills, which is invaluable for personal development and performance appraisals.

Case Study: Implementing Myers-Briggs Type Indicator (MBTI) in Management at Technology Company

Background: A leading technology firm faced challenges related to team dynamics and communication inefficiencies which impacted its project delivery timelines and overall workplace harmony. The management team hypothesized that a lack of understanding of individual personality types could be contributing to these challenges.

Objective: To improve team cohesion and enhance communication among team members by implementing the Myers-Briggs Type Indicator (MBTI) as a tool to understand and manage different personality types within the company. **Implementation:** TechCo partnered with a consulting firm specializing in organizational psychology to conduct MBTI workshops for all employees. The process included:

1. **Initial Assessment:**
   - All team members completed the MBTI assessment to identify their personality types.
   - Results were compiled and shared with both the individuals and their respective managers to foster a better understanding of personal and team dynamics.
2. **Workshop Sessions:**
   - Tailored workshops were conducted to explain the implications of different personality types and how they interact in a work setting.
   - Managers received specific training on adapting their management styles according to the diverse personality types in their teams.
3. **Integration into HR Practices:**
   - Incorporation of MBTI results into team formation strategies for projects.
   - Use of personality insights in conflict resolution and in tailoring communication for better clarity and reception.

Results: Over the course of the next year, the organisation observed significant improvements in several areas:

- **Enhanced Team Performance:**
  - ➢ Projects saw improved collaboration and a 30% reduction in delivery times due to more effective team compositions that considered personality compatibilities.
- **Reduced Conflict Rates:**
  - ➢ There was a noticeable 40% decrease in interpersonal conflicts as employees and managers better understood the diverse perspectives and communication styles influenced by different personality types.
- **Increased Employee Satisfaction:**
  - ➢ Employee satisfaction surveys indicated a 25% improvement in workplace satisfaction scores, with particular appreciation noted for the personal growth and understanding derived from the MBTI training.

Key Insights: This case demonstrates the profound impact that understanding personality types can have on managing a diverse workforce. Managers noted that recognizing the strengths and weaknesses typical of different MBTI profiles allowed them to assign tasks more effectively and manage expectations more realistically. One manager remarked, "Understanding the MBTI profiles has been akin to unlocking a new level of potential within our teams. It's not just about knowing who prefers to lead or follow; it's about creating an environment where everyone feels they are heard and valued."

Conclusion: This initiative at the organization underscores the relevance of personality assessment tools like MBTI in enhancing managerial effectiveness and improving team dynamics. The success seen in implementation of MBTI illustrates how tailored management strategies, grounded in psychological insights, can lead to substantial improvements in productivity, employee engagement, and overall organizational health.

Future Steps: Encouraged by these positive outcomes, the organisation plans to continue integrating personality assessments into their regular training programs and to explore additional tools that complement the MBTI to deepen their understanding of employee behaviors and preferences. This strategic approach to management, informed by psychological insights, is set to remain a cornerstone of the organizational development strategy.

Case Study: Enhancing Leadership Effectiveness at a Financial Corporation through Big Five Personality Traits Assessment

Background: A prominent financial services company faced challenges with leadership effectiveness and team cohesion. The executive team observed varying levels of performance and satisfaction across departments, which they suspected might be linked to mismatches between managerial styles and team needs.

Objective: To enhance leadership effectiveness and improve team cohesion by implementing the Big Five Personality Traits assessment across all managerial levels within the company.

Implementation: The financial corporation initiated a comprehensive program to assess the personality traits of its leaders using the Big Five Personality Traits framework, which includes Openness, Conscientiousness, Extraversion, Agreeableness, and Neuroticism. The process involved the following steps:

1. **Personality Assessment:**
   - All managers underwent evaluations to identify their dominant traits according to the Big Five framework.
   - Results were analyzed to understand the prevailing leadership styles within the company and their alignment with team dynamics.
2. **Training and Development Workshops:**
   - Customized workshops were designed to help leaders understand their own personality profiles and the profiles of their team members.
   - Leaders were trained on how to leverage their strengths and mitigate any weaknesses identified through the personality assessments.
3. **Strategic Leadership Re-alignment:**
   - Based on assessment results, some leadership realignments were made to better match managerial styles with team needs, particularly in areas where departmental performance was lagging.

- Ongoing support and coaching were provided to ensure a smooth transition and to foster new leadership approaches.

Results: Over the next 18 months, they experienced significant improvements:

- **Leadership Effectiveness:**
  - ➢ Leaders with high Agreeableness and Conscientiousness were paired with teams requiring steady guidance and reliability, leading to a 20% improvement in team performance metrics.
  - ➢ Departments under leaders with high Openness experienced enhanced innovation outputs, reflecting a 25% increase in the number of new initiatives successfully launched.
- **Employee Satisfaction:**
  - ➢ Annual employee satisfaction surveys showed a 30% improvement in scores related to leadership effectiveness and workplace harmony.
  - ➢ Employee turnover rates decreased by 15%, particularly in departments where leadership realignments had been implemented.
- **Organizational Impact:**
  - ➢ The overall productivity of FinCorp increased by 18%, with marked improvements in customer satisfaction and service delivery.
  - ➢ The initiative fostered a culture of self-awareness and developmental growth, enhancing the company's reputation as an employer of choice.

Key Insights: The application of the Big Five Personality Traits assessment revealed critical insights into how different personality dimensions influence leadership effectiveness and team dynamics. One senior executive noted, "The clarity gained from understanding our own personality traits and those of our colleagues has been transformative. It has not only improved how we lead but also how we collaborate as a team."

Conclusion: This initiative at Financial Corporation underscores the value of personality assessments in optimizing leadership within an organization. By aligning leadership styles with team needs and fostering an environment of mutual understanding and respect, companies can achieve substantial improvements in performance, employee satisfaction, and overall organizational health.

Future Steps: Encouraged by these positive outcomes, Financial Corporation plans to integrate personality assessments into their regular leadership development programs and extend this approach to all incoming managerial staff to maintain alignment and drive continuous improvement in leadership practices across the organization.

Chapter–3

Cognitive Process and Decision Making

"The world as we have created it is a process of our thinking. It cannot be changed without changing our thinking." – Albert Einstein

Understanding cognitive processes and decision-making is essential for effective management as it provides insights into how individuals perceive, process, and act upon information in the workplace. By delving into cognitive processes such as attention, memory, and problem-solving, managers can gain a deeper understanding of how their employees approach tasks, make decisions, and solve problems. This knowledge is invaluable for optimizing work processes, fostering innovation, and enhancing overall organizational performance.

How Managers Process Information

1. **Information Gathering**: Managers often begin by collecting data relevant to the decision at hand. This can involve seeking out both quantitative data, such as sales reports and financial statements, and qualitative data, such as employee feedback and customer reviews.

2. **Information Processing**: Once information is gathered, managers must process this data to make sense of it. This involves organizing the information, identifying relationships between different data points, and prioritizing what is most relevant to the decision-making process.
3. **Critical Thinking and Analysis**: Managers apply critical thinking to analyze the information. This step is vital to discern patterns, evaluate the validity of the data, and make predictions based on trends. It is here that cognitive biases can most influence decision-making, as personal experiences, values, and preferences may affect interpretation.
4. **Decision Execution**: After processing and analyzing the information, managers make a decision and proceed to implement it. This often requires careful planning to manage resources effectively and to communicate the decision to those it affects, ensuring alignment and understanding within the team.

Common Cognitive Biases and How to Mitigate Them

Cognitive biases are systematic patterns of deviation from norm or rationality in judgment, whereby inferences about other people and situations may be drawn in an illogical fashion. Here are some common biases and strategies to mitigate them:

1. **Confirmation Bias**: This is the tendency to search for, interpret, favor, and recall information in a way that confirms one's preexisting beliefs or hypotheses.

To counteract this, managers should actively seek out information that challenges their assumptions and consider alternative viewpoints.

2. **Anchoring Bias**: This occurs when individuals rely too heavily on the first piece of information they receive. To avoid this, managers should ensure they consider additional data and perspectives before making a decision.
3. **Overconfidence Bias**: This bias leads individuals to overestimate their own abilities, which can result in taking greater risks. Managers should regularly solicit feedback and encourage a culture of open communication where employees feel comfortable voicing opinions and concerns.
4. **Availability Heuristic**: This is a mental shortcut that relies on immediate examples that come to a given person's mind when evaluating a specific topic, concept, method or decision. To mitigate this, managers should base their decisions on more comprehensive data rather than just the information that is most readily available.

Decision-Making Models and Their Application in Management

1. **Rational Decision-Making Model**: This model involves identifying the problem, gathering information, evaluating the alternatives, making the choice, implementing the decision, and reviewing the results. It assumes a logical and orderly process and is most effective when decisions are complex and require detailed analysis.

2. **Intuitive Decision-Making Model**: Sometimes referred to as the 'gut feeling', intuitive decision-making can be faster than rational processes and is often used when time is limited. Managers using this model rely on their experiences and emotions to guide their choices. While this can be effective, it is also susceptible to biases.
3. **Incremental Model**: This model involves taking small steps towards a decision. It is particularly useful in situations where the outcome is uncertain, and risks need to be minimized. This approach allows managers to adjust their path as new information becomes available.
4. **Group Decision-Making**: Often used to draw on the diverse skills and experiences of a team, this model can enhance decision quality. However, it requires effective communication and conflict resolution skills to manage differing opinions and reach a consensus.

Part–II

Psychological Approaches to Management

Chapter–4

Leadership Psychology

"Emotional intelligence matters for leadership effectiveness, as it enables leaders to understand and navigate the emotions of themselves and others, fostering a more empathetic and impactful leadership approach."
–Daniel Goleman

Understanding Leadership Psychology encompasses a multifaceted exploration of the psychological traits of effective leaders, the diverse spectrum of leadership styles, and the contemporary significance of emotional intelligence (EQ) in the present day. Psychological traits such as self-awareness, empathy, and humility are paramount for effective leadership, fostering authentic influence and trust within teams. Leadership styles, ranging from transformational to situational, offer insights into the diverse approaches that leaders can adopt to inspire and guide their teams. Moreover, the importance of EQ in leadership cannot be overstated, as it correlates with job performance and is a critical component of effective leadership.

Psychological Traits of Effective Leaders

1. **Self-Awareness**:
    - **Critical Importance**: Leaders with high self-awareness are better equipped to handle organizational challenges. They understand their personal impact on others and can adjust their behavior accordingly.
    - **Development Strategies**: Regular feedback sessions, reflective practices, and even professional coaching can enhance a leader's self-awareness.
2. **Resilience**:
    - **Role in Leadership**: Resilience allows leaders to endure difficult times with grace, and to emerge from challenges stronger than before.
    - **Building Resilience**: This can be developed through stress management training, scenario planning, and fostering a supportive network.
3. **Integrity**:
    - **Foundation of Trust**: Integrity in leadership fosters an environment of trust and safety, which is essential for open communication and team cohesion.
    - **Maintaining Integrity**: Consistently demonstrating ethical behaviors and making transparent decisions are crucial.
4. **Adaptability**:
    - **Navigating Change**: The ability to adapt to changing situations is indispensable in today's fast-paced business environment.

- **Enhancing Adaptability**: Leaders can become more adaptable by seeking diverse experiences, learning continuously, and being open to new ideas.

5. **Vision**:

- **Inspiring a Shared Future**: A clear and compelling vision helps align and motivate the team towards common goals.
- **Articulating Vision**: Effective communication skills are necessary to articulate a vision that is both inspiring and understandable.

Leadership Styles and Their Psychological Impacts

1. **Transformational Leadership**:

- **Empowering Employees**: This style is particularly effective in environments that require innovation and change. Leaders who can inspire and motivate their teams not only achieve high levels of performance but also drive organizational transformation.
- **Psychological Effects**: Increases job satisfaction and organizational commitment among team members.

2. **Transactional Leadership**:

- **Reward-based Motivation**: While effective in achieving short-term goals, this style may not be as successful in environments that require flexibility and creativity.
- **When to Use**: Best employed in situations where specific standards and procedures need to be followed.

3. **Servant Leadership**:
   - **Focus on Team Needs**: By prioritizing the needs of the team, servant leaders enhance employee morale and engagement.
   - **Long-term Benefits**: Often results in higher levels of trust, increased cooperation, and stronger team loyalty.
4. **Autocratic Leadership**:
   - **Direct Decision Making**: Useful in crisis situations where rapid, decisive action is needed.
   - **Limitations**: May lead to reduced employee morale and creativity if used excessively.
5. **Democratic Leadership**:
   - **Inclusive Approach**: Encourages team involvement in decision-making, which can enhance solution quality and team satisfaction.
   - **Appropriate Contexts**: Most effective in knowledge-intensive environments or when complex problems require diverse input.

Emotional Intelligence and Its Significance in Leadership

Emotional Intelligence (EI) has emerged as a vital component in the realm of leadership, transcending traditional notions that prioritize technical skills and intellectual prowess alone. This segment delves into the essence of emotional intelligence and explores its profound significance in effective leadership.

Understanding Emotional Intelligence

1. Definition and Components:

- **Emotional intelligence** refers to the capacity to recognize, understand, manage, and reason with emotions, both in oneself and in others.
- EI comprises four primary components:
  - **Self-awareness**: Recognizing one's own emotions and their effects.
  - **Self-regulation**: Managing or redirecting one's disruptive emotions and adapting to changing circumstances.
  - **Empathy**: Understanding, recognizing, and considering other people's emotions, a critical aspect of effective leadership.
  - **Social skills**: Managing relationships to move people in desired directions, whether in negotiating, leading a team, or managing a conflict.

2. Theoretical Background:

- Pioneered by psychologists John Mayer and Peter Salovey, and later popularized by Daniel Goleman, the concept of EI has become integral in understanding the dynamics of effective leadership.
- Goleman's model links emotional intelligence directly to measurable business outcomes, highlighting its importance not just in personal well-being but also in achieving professional success.

Significance of Emotional Intelligence in Leadership

1. **Enhanced Leadership Effectiveness**:
   - Leaders with high EI are adept at sensing team emotions, enabling them to manage situations tactfully and inspire and motivate their teams efficiently.
   - As Goleman posits, "The most effective leaders are all alike in one crucial way: they all have a high degree of emotional intelligence."
2. **Improved Communication and Relationship Management**:
   - Emotional intelligence facilitates open communication and fosters a strong leader-follower relationship. Leaders who show empathy can better engage their employees and earn their trust and respect.
   - This rapport not only improves team morale but also drives the alignment of personal goals with organizational objectives.
3. **Conflict Resolution**:
   - The ability to empathetically and objectively manage and resolve conflicts is a direct benefit of high EI.
   - Leaders who can navigate through conflicts constructively can maintain a positive team dynamic and prevent potential disruptions.
4. **Adaptability to Change**:
   - Change is constant in any business setting, and leaders with high emotional intelligence are better

equipped to handle change. Their ability to manage their own and others' emotions helps them guide their teams through transitions smoothly.

5. **Talent Retention**:

   - By creating a supportive and understanding work environment, emotionally intelligent leaders help reduce staff turnover and attract top talent. Their leadership style promotes an inclusive culture that values and nurtures its members.

Developing Emotional Intelligence

1. **Self-Assessment and Reflection**:

   - Regular self-assessment of emotional strengths and weaknesses can help leaders identify areas for improvement. Reflective practices such as journaling or meditation can aid in developing a deeper level of self-awareness.

2. **Feedback and Coaching**:

   - Constructive feedback from peers, mentors, or coaches can provide valuable insights into how a leader's emotional behavior impacts others.
   - Emotional intelligence coaching is another effective method for enhancing a leader's ability to understand and manage emotions.

3. **Training Programs**:

   - Many organizations now offer training programs focused on developing emotional competencies. These programs often include practical exercises designed to improve empathy, emotional regulation, and interpersonal skills.

4. **Practical Application**:

- Applying emotional intelligence concepts in everyday interactions is crucial. Leaders should practice active listening, show genuine interest in team members, and provide support where needed.

Chapter–5

Motivation and Engagement

"Motivation is the art of getting people to do what you want them to do because they want to do it." – *William Butler*

Understanding motivation and engagement is pivotal for nurturing a high-performing and fulfilled workforce. Motivation serves as the driving force behind employee performance, influencing their dedication, productivity, and commitment to organizational goals. Employee engagement, on the other hand, is vital for creating a work environment where employees feel connected to their work, their colleagues, and the organization's mission, resulting in increased productivity, innovation, and job satisfaction.

Theories of Motivation: Exploring Maslow's Hierarchy of Needs and Herzberg's Two-Factor Theory

Motivation theories are crucial for understanding what drives human behavior, particularly in the workplace. This detailed exploration focuses on two foundational theories: Maslow's Hierarchy of Needs and Herzberg's Two-Factor Theory, providing insights into how these theories can be applied to enhance employee motivation and organizational effectiveness.

Maslow's Hierarchy of Needs

Overview: Developed by Abraham Maslow in the 1940s, this theory is often visualized as a pyramid consisting of five levels of needs. Maslow proposed that individuals are motivated to fulfill basic needs before moving on to higher-level needs. **The Five Levels:**

1. Physiological Needs:

- These are the basic, biological necessities of life, such as food, water, and shelter.
- In a workplace context, this translates to adequate wages that cover life's essentials.

2. Safety Needs:

- Once physiological needs are met, the focus shifts to safety and security.
- Employees seek stability in their job, safe working conditions, and protection from physical and emotional harm.

3. Social Needs:

- These involve the need for belonging and love. People need to feel accepted and appreciated by their peers and superiors.
- Creating a supportive team environment and fostering good relationships can satisfy these needs.

4. Esteem Needs:

- After social needs are fulfilled, individuals desire respect, self-esteem, and personal worth.

- Recognition, high-status positions, and awards can motivate employees by fulfilling these needs.

5. Self-Actualization Needs:

- This is the highest level of Maslow's hierarchy and involves realizing one's own potential and self-fulfillment.
- Opportunities for personal growth, creativity, and advancement allow employees to reach self-actualization.

Application in Management: Understanding Maslow's theory helps managers ensure that the needs of employees are met at each level. As Maslow himself noted, "What a man can be, he must be. This need we call self-actualization." By facilitating the fulfillment of these needs, managers can foster a motivated, efficient, and loyal workforce.

Herzberg's Two-Factor Theory

Overview: Developed by Frederick Herzberg in the 1950s, this theory distinguishes between factors that cause job satisfaction and those that cause dissatisfaction, known as 'Hygiene' and 'Motivator' factors, respectively. **Key Components:**

1. Hygiene Factors:

- These are factors that do not lead to higher motivation but, if absent, cause dissatisfaction.
- Examples include salary, work conditions, company policies, and job security.
- Managers must ensure that hygiene factors are adequately addressed to prevent employee dissatisfaction.

2. Motivator Factors:

- These factors truly motivate employees, leading to higher performance and satisfaction.
- They include aspects such as recognition, achievement, and personal growth.
- Herzberg emphasized that fulfilling these needs can encourage employees to excel beyond average expectations and achieve their full potential.

Application in Management: Herzberg's theory suggests that simply removing dissatisfaction is not enough to motivate employees. Instead, enhancing motivator factors is key. "If you want someone to do a good job, give them a good job to do," as Herzberg famously stated. This means providing challenging, meaningful work and recognizing achievements in a way that fulfills employees' higher-level needs.

Techniques for Enhancing Employee Motivation and Engagement

Employee motivation and engagement are pivotal to the success of any organization. Engaged employees are more productive, deliver higher quality work, and are less likely to leave the organization. This detailed exploration discusses various techniques to enhance employee motivation and engagement effectively.

Understanding Employee Needs

1. Tailored Approach:

- Recognize that each employee is unique with distinct motivational drivers. Personalizing engagement strategies to meet individual needs can significantly boost motivation.

- Techniques include personalized development plans, flexible working options, and recognition that aligns with personal values and preferences.

2. **Communication and Feedback**:

- Regular, open communication channels between employees and management help in understanding and addressing their needs effectively.
- Implementing continuous feedback mechanisms, rather than annual reviews, ensures timely recognition of efforts and constructive guidance on areas for improvement.

Creating a Positive Work Environment

1. **Inclusive Culture**:

- Foster an inclusive and respectful workplace culture that encourages collaboration and open communication.
- Activities like team-building exercises and social events can enhance interpersonal relationships and create a more cohesive work environment.

2. **Safe and Healthy Workplace**:

- Ensure that the physical workplace is safe, comfortable, and conducive to productivity.
- Promoting mental health awareness and support, providing ergonomic workstations, and ensuring health and safety standards can significantly impact employee well-being and motivation.

Recognition and Rewards

1. **Regular Recognition**:
   - Frequent acknowledgment of employees' hard work and achievements can significantly boost morale and motivation.
   - Techniques include public recognition, awards, and informal thank-yous that make employees feel valued and appreciated.
2. **Performance-Based Rewards**:
   - Aligning rewards with performance not only motivates high achievers but also sets a benchmark for others.
   - Options include bonuses, salary raises, promotions, or non-monetary rewards like extra holidays or professional development opportunities.

Professional Growth and Development

1. **Career Advancement Opportunities**:
   - Employees are more motivated when they see a clear path for career advancement within the organization.
   - Providing structured career development plans, mentoring programs, and access to training and education can empower employees and foster loyalty.
2. **Skill Development**:
   - Investing in employees' professional skills not only benefits the organization but also contributes to the individual's career growth.

- Workshops, seminars, and access to courses related to their field can enhance their skill set and keep them engaged and motivated.

Empowerment and Autonomy

1. Decision-Making Power:

- Empowering employees by involving them in decision-making processes can enhance their commitment and satisfaction.
- Techniques include participative management styles where employees are encouraged to contribute ideas and make decisions relevant to their work.

2. Autonomy in Work:

- Granting employees autonomy in how they complete their tasks provides them with a sense of ownership and responsibility.
- This can be facilitated by setting clear goals and performance metrics while giving them the freedom to achieve these in their way.

Leveraging Technology

1. Digital Tools for Engagement:

- Utilize technology to create more engaging and efficient work processes.
- Tools like project management software, instant messaging platforms, and employee engagement apps can streamline workflows and enhance communication.

2. Remote Working Technologies:

- With the rise of remote work, providing employees

with the necessary tools to work effectively from any location is crucial.

- This includes reliable communication tools, access to cloud services, and robust cybersecurity measures to facilitate a flexible work environment.

Employee Engagement Strategies and Their Psychological Foundations

Employee engagement is a vital aspect of organizational success, influencing everything from productivity to retention. Understanding the psychological foundations behind engagement strategies can help organizations create more effective policies and practices that foster a committed and satisfied workforce.

Psychological Foundations of Engagement

1. **Cognitive Evaluation Theory**:
   - This theory suggests that extrinsic rewards can reduce intrinsic interest in a task. For engagement strategies, this means balancing tangible rewards with opportunities for intrinsic satisfaction, such as personal growth and recognition.
   - **Application**: Design job roles that provide meaningful work, autonomy, and opportunities to master skills, rather than focusing solely on bonuses and pay raises.
2. **Self-Determination Theory (SDT)**:
   - SDT emphasizes three fundamental psychological needs: competence, autonomy, and relatedness. When these needs are satisfied, higher motivation and engagement are likely.

- **Application**: Implement policies that empower employees, foster a sense of belonging, and enable skill development to enhance overall job satisfaction and engagement.

3. **Social Exchange Theory**:
   - This theory posits that relationships are formed based on a reciprocal exchange process. In the workplace, if employees feel the organization values and invests in them, they are more likely to reciprocate with loyalty and engagement.
   - **Application**: Cultivate a supportive work environment that values employee contributions, provides fair compensation, and recognizes efforts to encourage a deeper commitment to the organization.

Strategies for Enhancing Employee Engagement

1. **Transparent Communication**:
   - Open lines of communication build trust and help employees feel valued and understood.
   - **Psychological Insight**: According to Maslow's hierarchy, social needs and esteem are critical for motivation. Regular, transparent communication addresses these needs by making employees feel part of a community and respected.
2. **Recognition and Reward Systems**:
   - Tailored recognition programs that celebrate both small wins and major accomplishments can significantly boost morale.

- **Psychological Insight**: Herzberg's Two-Factor Theory highlights recognition as a key motivator. Effective recognition satisfies employees' need for esteem and acknowledgment, directly impacting their engagement levels.

3. **Professional Development Opportunities**:
   - Continuous learning and development initiatives keep employees engaged by helping them advance their skills and careers.
   - **Psychological Insight**: The principle of self-actualization from Maslow's theory and the need for competence in SDT suggest that opportunities for personal and professional growth can enhance engagement.

4. **Flexible Work Arrangements**:
   - Flexibility in work schedules and locations can lead to a better work-life balance, reducing stress and increasing job satisfaction.
   - **Psychological Insight**: Autonomy is a core component of SDT. Flexible work arrangements provide employees with a sense of control over their work and personal lives, boosting their engagement and satisfaction.

5. **Employee Wellness Programs**:
   - Comprehensive wellness programs that address physical, mental, and emotional health can improve overall employee well-being and engagement.
   - **Psychological Insight**: According to SDT, relatedness and feeling cared for are crucial for

psychological well-being. Wellness programs demonstrate organizational care and concern, fulfilling these psychological needs.

6. **Inclusive Culture and Diversity**:
   - Promoting an inclusive culture where diversity is celebrated can enhance employee engagement by creating a sense of belonging and safety.
   - **Psychological Insight**: Social identity theory explains how group membership can influence self-esteem and behavior. An inclusive workplace where employees feel a strong sense of group identity can increase engagement and loyalty.
7. **Feedback Mechanisms**:
   - Regular and constructive feedback helps employees understand their performance and areas for improvement, fostering a culture of transparency and growth.
   - **Psychological Insight**: Feedback addresses the need for competence and esteem. It helps employees feel valued and provides clear pathways for improvement, which are crucial for engagement.

Chapter–6

Communication and Interpersonal Relations

Understanding communication and interpersonal relations is foundational for fostering a harmonious and productive work environment. Effective communication skills are paramount for conveying ideas, resolving conflicts, and building strong professional relationships. Conflict is an inevitable aspect of interpersonal relations, and the ability to navigate and resolve conflicts is crucial for maintaining a positive work environment. As highlighted in "Communication in the Real World," "Remember that it's not the quantity of conflict that determines a relationship's success; it's how the conflict is managed, and one person's competent response can de-escalate a conflict." This quote underscores the significance of conflict management skills in fostering effective communication and maintaining healthy interpersonal relationships within the workplace.

Furthermore, building professional relationships through effective communication fosters a sense of trust, collaboration, and mutual understanding among team members. It enables individuals to connect on a deeper level, fostering a supportive and cohesive work environment. By prioritizing open and transparent communication, individuals can navigate challenges, share ideas, and build a strong network of professional relationships, ultimately contributing to a more positive and productive organizational culture.

Psychological Barriers to Effective Communication

Understanding psychological barriers to effective communication is crucial for fostering a productive and harmonious work environment. These barriers, often rooted in individual perceptions and emotional states, can significantly distort message transmission and reception.

Emotional Barriers: Emotions profoundly influence how we communicate and interpret messages. For instance, anger or frustration can lead to aggressive communication or misinterpretation of messages, which may cause conflict or misunderstanding. Similarly, anxiety might prevent individuals from expressing their thoughts clearly, leading to confusion and miscommunication. Managing emotional responses and striving for emotional neutrality in discussions can help mitigate these barriers.

Perceptual Barriers: Perception plays a critical role in communication. Each individual perceives information through the lens of their personal experiences, biases, and beliefs. This subjective view can lead to different interpretations of the same message, potentially causing miscommunication. For example, a simple comment may be perceived as criticism depending on the listener's self-esteem or past experiences. To overcome perceptual barriers, it is essential to seek clarity by asking questions and paraphrasing to ensure understanding.

Cultural Barriers: In an increasingly globalized world, cultural differences can significantly impact communication. Variations in communication styles, expressions, and understanding of verbal and non-verbal cues can lead to misinterpretations. For instance, direct communication styles common in some cultures may be perceived as rude in others that value indirect communication. Awareness and sensitivity to cultural differences are vital, and adopting a culturally informed communication style can enhance clarity and reduce misunderstandings.

Language Barriers: Even when communicating in the same language, differences in terminology, jargon, and colloquial expressions can obstruct effective communication. Specialist jargon and abbreviations familiar to one group may be entirely alien to another, leading to confusion. Clear and simple language, free from unnecessary jargon, can help bridge this gap, making communication more accessible to all participants.

Psychological Noise: Distractions that affect the mental state of the communicator can also be significant barriers. Psychological noise includes preoccupations, worries, or stress unrelated to the communication at hand but that affect the focus and mental clarity of the communicator. Recognizing and addressing these distractions can improve the effectiveness of communication. Techniques such as mindfulness and ensuring a distraction-free environment during important communications can be beneficial.

Attitudes and Biases: Preconceived notions and attitudes towards certain topics or individuals can skew rational and objective communication. Biases can lead to assumptions that cloud judgment and interpretation. Being aware of one's biases and actively working to set them aside when communicating can lead to more effective and impartial communication.

Interpersonal Relations: The dynamics of interpersonal relationships can also act as barriers. For instance, if there is a history of conflict between individuals, communication may be strained, and messages may be interpreted with bias. Building positive interpersonal relationships through trust and respect can help minimize these barriers. Effective communication requires an understanding of these psychological barriers and a concerted effort to overcome them. Techniques such as active listening, empathetic engagement, and clear, respectful expression can help navigate these barriers. As highlighted by the complexity of human interactions, effective communication is not merely about exchanging information but also about understanding the emotional and psychological contexts in which this information is exchanged.

Conflict Resolution Strategies

Conflict resolution is an essential skill in any organizational setting, where diverse opinions and personalities can often lead to disputes. Effective conflict resolution strategies not only prevent potential escalations but also transform conflicts into productive discussions. Understanding and implementing these strategies can significantly enhance workplace harmony and productivity.

Active Listening

Active listening involves fully concentrating on the speaker, understanding their message, and responding thoughtfully. It forms the foundation of effective conflict resolution by ensuring that all parties feel heard and understood, which is crucial in de-escalating tensions.

Example: During a team meeting at a marketing firm, two team members disagreed on the direction of a new campaign. The team leader intervened, asking each member to articulate the other's point of view before responding. This exercise helped clarify misunderstandings and opened a pathway to a compromise that incorporated both ideas.

Assertiveness and Empathy

Balancing assertiveness with empathy allows individuals to express their views clearly and respectfully while considering others' perspectives. This approach respects all parties' needs and can lead to more sustainable resolutions.

Example: In a project management scenario, a team member felt overwhelmed with her workload and was unable to meet deadlines, causing tension. By assertively expressing her limits and empathetically understanding her team's goals, she and her manager could reallocate some tasks, thus resolving the conflict without resentment.

Seeking Common Ground

Focusing on shared interests rather than differences can help de-escalate conflicts. By identifying common goals, parties involved can shift from opposing positions to collaborative problem-solving.

Example: Two IT departments were clashing over budget allocations for new software. By focusing on the shared goal of technological advancement for the company, they agreed to jointly present a case for increased funding from upper management rather than competing for existing resources.

Addressing Conflicts Early

Proactively addressing signs of conflict can prevent them from escalating into more significant issues. Early intervention also helps maintain trust and respect among team members.

Example: Noticing increased frustration during team interactions, a department head scheduled a mediation session to address issues before they intensified. The early discussion helped clarify communication breakdowns and adjusted expectations that aligned with team capabilities.

Mediation and Facilitation

Involving a neutral third party can help mediate discussions and facilitate a fair resolution, especially in more severe conflicts. This person can help maintain objectivity and ensure that all voices are heard.

Example: During a merger, two companies faced significant cultural clashes. An external mediator was brought in to facilitate integration workshops where employees from both companies could express their concerns and expectations. The mediator helped both groups understand each other's corporate cultures and work towards a unified organizational culture.

Scheduled Conflict Resolution

Sometimes, it is beneficial to acknowledge a conflict but postpone the discussion until all parties are less emotionally charged. This approach allows time for reflection and can lead to more rational and less confrontational interactions.

Example: After a heated disagreement in a board meeting, the chairperson proposed that the discussion be continued the following day to allow everyone to cool down and consider the issues more carefully. The subsequent meeting was more productive, with participants offering constructive solutions instead of arguing.

Use of Humor

Appropriately used, humor can lighten the mood and open up people to more flexible thinking, which can be helpful in resolving conflicts. However, it must be used sensitively and appropriately to avoid minimizing serious concerns.

Example: In a tense meeting where team members were arguing over the allocation of office space, the manager joked that at least they weren't fighting over something trivial like office supplies. This comment made everyone laugh and reduced the tension, making it easier to discuss practical solutions. Effective conflict resolution requires a combination of understanding, tact, and timely intervention. By employing these strategies, organizations can foster a more collaborative and supportive work environment, turning potential conflicts into opportunities for growth and innovation. As the saying goes, "Peace is not absence of conflict, it is the ability to handle conflict by peaceful means." — Ronald Reagan.

Building and Maintaining Professional Relationships

Strong professional relationships are the backbone of successful teams and organizations.

1. **Consistent Communication**: Regular and open communication is essential. It builds trust, clarifies expectations, and fosters a strong collaborative spirit.
2. **Respect and Trust**: Mutual respect and trust form the foundation of all strong relationships. These qualities are earned through consistent, fair, and reliable behavior.
3. **Recognition and Appreciation**: Regularly recognizing and appreciating each other's efforts strengthens relationships and boosts morale. This can be as simple as thanking a colleague for their help or celebrating team achievements.
4. **Networking and Socializing**: Informal interactions outside of regular work tasks can deepen relationships. Social events, team-building activities, and professional networking help strengthen bonds.
5. **Feedback and Personal Development**: Constructive feedback is a gift that can help individuals grow. Offering and receiving feedback graciously is a critical skill in maintaining healthy professional relationships.

By investing in these areas, organizations can cultivate a work environment where communication flourishes and relationships thrive, leading to increased productivity and job satisfaction. As the adage goes, "People do business with people they know, like, and trust."

Part–III

Organizational Behavior and Culture

Chapter–7

Team Dynamics

Understanding team dynamics encompasses the intricate processes of team formation, development, and the management of diverse and cross-functional teams. The trajectory of team mates during each stage of the Tuckman team formation model and the DISC theory, which predicts behaviors based on key personality traits, provide valuable insights into conflict management and the establishment of trust as a crucial first step in managing conflict, achieving commitment, creating accountability, and focusing on results. Additionally, understanding the temporal dimensions of team processes, such as task cycles and linear development, is essential for aligning team processes with task demands and fostering skill acquisition and development. Managing diverse and cross-functional teams involves leveraging the diverse and complementary strengths, talents, education, and experience of team members to create a cohesive and high-performing unit, ultimately contributing to the organization's success.

Psychological Aspects of Team Formation and Development

Understanding the psychological aspects of team formation and development is essential for fostering effective teamwork and achieving organizational goals. The dynamics of team development are complex, involving various stages where psychological factors play a critical role.

Stages of Team Development

Bruce Tuckman's model of team development, established in 1965 and later expanded, outlines five key stages that teams typically undergo. Each stage presents unique challenges and opportunities for psychological growth and team cohesion.

1. **Forming**: In this initial stage, team members are introduced. They cautiously explore the boundaries of acceptable group behavior. This is a stage of orientation, where individuals are coming together for the first time and are keen on making a good impression. It's characterized by a degree of uncertainty and anxiety as members are not yet aware of the exact dynamics and expectations.

2. **Storming**: This stage is marked by conflict and competition as personal relations are defined. Team members start to push against the boundaries established in the forming stage. This phase can be contentious as personalities clash and people vie for positions and status within the team. The storming stage is crucial for the growth of the team, although it's often uncomfortable and fraught with conflict.

3. **Norming**: Once teams navigate the storming stage, they enter the norming phase where consensus develops, roles are accepted, and expectations are solidified. Team members reconcile competing loyalties and responsibilities. They accept the team, team rules, their roles in the team, and the idiosyncrasies of their fellow members. The norming stage is where a cohesive unit begins to materialize, and more profound connections develop.
4. **Performing**: The team finally starts working as a cohesive unit, aiming towards the team's goals and achieving more with less friction. Members are competent, autonomous, and able to handle the decision-making process without supervision. Interdependence is achieved, and the team becomes fully functional.
5. **Adjourning**: Tuckman's final stage, adjourning involves the disassembly of the team after the objective has been achieved. This stage is often overlooked but is crucial for psychological closure, particularly in project teams. Members may experience uncertainty and grief as they disengage and separate from the team.

Psychological Dynamics in Each Stage

Each stage of team development is influenced by underlying psychological dynamics:

- **Forming**: The primary psychological challenge is the fear of the unknown and the desire to be accepted by others. Team leaders can facilitate this stage by being clear about team goals and expected behaviors.

- **Storming**: The psychological focus here is on individuals' struggle to reconcile their personal goals with the team's goals. Effective communication and conflict resolution skills are crucial in this stage to mediate tensions.
- **Norming**: Developing a sense of unity and cohesion is the psychological underpinning of this stage. Leaders can foster this by encouraging team traditions and shared values.
- **Performing**: High levels of trust and communication are the psychological pillars of this stage. Team members feel confident and motivated to perform at their best.
- **Adjourning**: Recognition of the team's work and reflection on individual growth are important for psychological closure. Celebrating the team's achievements can ease the transition and provide a sense of completion and satisfaction.

Understanding these psychological aspects of team dynamics helps leaders and managers to effectively guide their teams through the complexities of group development. By recognizing the needs and behaviors characteristic of each stage, they can implement strategies to better support their teams, ultimately leading to more successful and harmonious collaborations. As teams evolve through these stages, they build resilience and flexibility, becoming more adept at navigating internal and external challenges

The Role of Groupthink, Conformity, and Other Group Processes in Management

In the realm of organizational behavior, understanding group dynamics such as groupthink, conformity, and other group processes is essential for effective management. These phenomena can significantly influence team decision-making and productivity, either positively or negatively.

Groupthink

Groupthink occurs when a group values harmony and coherence over accurate analysis and optimal decision-making. It leads to poor decision outcomes as the desire for consensus overrides the motivation to appraise alternative courses of action.

1. **Symptoms of Groupthink**:
   - **Illusion of Invulnerability**: Creating excessive optimism and encouraging risk-taking.
   - **Collective Rationalization**: Dismissing warnings that might challenge the group's assumptions.
   - **Belief in Inherent Morality**: Believing in the rightness of their cause, which ignores the ethical or moral consequences of decisions.
   - **Stereotyped Views of Out-Groups**: Negative views of "enemy" groups seen as too evil to negotiate with or too weak to defend themselves against.
2. **Preventing Groupthink**:
   - **Encourage Open Debate**: Assign the role of a devil's advocate to challenge the consensus and offer differing viewpoints.

- **Diverse Teams**: Include people from diverse backgrounds to provide a range of perspectives.
- **Independent Research**: Encourage team members to critically evaluate all alternatives and seek external opinions to inform their views.

Conformity

Conformity in organizational settings is the act of matching attitudes, beliefs, and behaviors to what individuals perceive as the norm of the group. While it can foster coordination and synchrony, excessive conformity can stifle innovation and individual accountability.

1. **Causes of Conformity**:
    - **Normative Influence**: The desire to fit in with the group to be liked or accepted.
    - **Informational Influence**: Conforming because the group is believed to be more knowledgeable or correct.
2. **Managing Conformity**:
    - **Promote a Culture of Questioning**: Encourage employees to question norms and speak up without fear of repercussions.
    - **Reward Innovation**: Recognize and reward employees who bring new ideas and challenge the status quo, reinforcing that creative dissent is valued.

Other Group Processes

Other significant group processes include social loafing, polarization, and synergy, each playing a unique role in group dynamics and management.

1. **Social Loafing**:
    - **Definition**: The phenomenon where individuals exert less effort to achieve a goal when they work in a group than when they work alone.
    - **Management Strategies**: Assign clear individual responsibilities and monitor individual contributions to ensure accountability.
2. **Group Polarization**:
    - **Definition**: The tendency for a group to make decisions that are more extreme than the initial inclination of its members.
    - **Management Strategies**: Expose the group to a wide range of views on the issue. This can prevent the group from shifting too far in a particular direction.
3. **Synergy**:
    - **Definition**: The creation of a whole that is greater than the simple sum of its parts. In a team setting, synergy occurs when group collaboration produces superior results than could be achieved by individual effort.
    - **Fostering Synergy**: Promote effective communication, mutual respect, and cohesive team-building activities that enhance trust and interdependence.

Managing Diverse and Cross-Functional Teams

Managing diverse and cross-functional teams is a complex yet rewarding endeavor that combines various skills, experiences, and cultural backgrounds to achieve a common objective. These teams are often more innovative and effective due to their varied perspectives, but they also present unique management challenges.

Understanding Cross-Functional Teams

A cross-functional team typically includes members from different departments or areas of expertise working together towards a shared goal. This could involve a mix of product managers, engineers, marketers, and customer support representatives, each bringing their specialized knowledge to the table. The diversity in skills and perspectives is intended to foster a holistic approach to projects, enhancing creativity and problem-solving capabilities.

Challenges of Managing Diverse Teams

1. **Communication Barriers**: Effective communication across different disciplines can be challenging. Each field has its own jargon and methodologies, which can lead to misunderstandings or misinterpretations. Overcoming this requires clear, jargon-free communication and regular team meetings to ensure all members are on the same page.

2. **Cultural Differences**: Teams that span multiple geographical locations encounter varied cultural perspectives that can influence work styles and interpersonal interactions. Managers must be culturally sensitive and promote inclusivity to harness these differences positively.

3. **Alignment of Goals**: Aligning the diverse goals and priorities of different departments can be

challenging. Without a clear, common objective, team efforts can become disjointed.

Strategies for Effective Management

1. **Leadership and Facilitation**: Effective leadership is crucial in managing cross-functional teams. Leaders must be facilitators, enabling each team member to contribute their expertise at the right time. This involves understanding the strengths and weaknesses of each team member and assigning tasks accordingly.

2. **Fostering Collaboration**: Encouraging a collaborative environment is essential. This can be achieved through team-building activities that enhance mutual respect and understanding, and by creating opportunities for informal interactions among team members.

3. **Utilizing Project Management Tools**: Leveraging technology to manage projects can significantly enhance efficiency and coordination. Project management tools help in tracking progress, distributing tasks, and maintaining communication among team members.

4. **Conflict Resolution**: With diversity comes the potential for conflict. Establishing clear protocols for conflict resolution ensures that disagreements are handled constructively. Regular feedback sessions and open communication channels can help in identifying and addressing issues early.

5. **Training and Development**: Providing training that focuses on cross-functional collaboration and

cultural competence can prepare team members for the challenges of working in diverse teams. This includes training in communication, negotiation, and conflict resolution skills.

6. **Recognition and Rewards**: Recognizing and rewarding the contributions of team members can motivate and encourage further collaboration and innovation. It's important that recognition is fair and inclusive, reflecting the contributions of all team members.

Benefits of Cross-Functional Teams

When managed effectively, cross-functional teams can drive significant benefits for an organization. They bring together diverse perspectives that can lead to more innovative solutions and products. They also break down silos within an organization, leading to improved communication and greater sharing of knowledge across departments.

Managing diverse and cross-functional teams requires a thoughtful approach that considers the complexities of different disciplines and cultural backgrounds. Effective management of these teams not only enhances productivity but also fosters a creative and inclusive workplace environment. As organizations continue to globalize and seek innovative solutions, the ability to lead such teams effectively will be increasingly valued.

Chapter–8

Organisational Structure and Culture

"Culture eats strategy for breakfast." – Peter Drucker

Understanding organizational structure and culture is pivotal for comprehending how organizational design influences employee behavior, the creation and management of organizational culture, and the psychological impact of organizational change. Organizational design significantly shapes employee behavior by delineating reporting relationships, communication channels, and decision-making processes. A hierarchical structure, for instance, may foster a more formal and controlled work environment, while a flat structure can promote autonomy and collaboration. Moreover, creating and managing organizational culture involves aligning values, beliefs, and behaviors with the organization's mission and goals. Leaders play a crucial role in shaping and nurturing the organizational culture, as it directly impacts employee engagement, job satisfaction, and overall performance. Additionally, the psychological impact of organizational change can be profound, often leading to uncertainty, resistance, and stress among employees. Managing organizational change effectively requires transparent communication, empathy, and involving employees in the change process to mitigate the psychological impact and facilitate a smoother transition.

How Organizational Design Affects Employee Behavior

Organizational design significantly influences employee behavior by shaping their daily experiences and interactions within the workplace. The structure of an organization determines the hierarchy, communication patterns, and the allocation of responsibilities, which in turn affect employee motivation, satisfaction, and performance.

Impact of Hierarchy and Control Structures

The hierarchy within an organization defines the levels of responsibility and the chain of command. A strict hierarchy can provide clear directives and simplify decision-making processes, but it may also limit the scope for employee autonomy and innovation. In contrast, a flatter organizational structure tends to promote greater openness and fluid communication, fostering an environment where employees feel more empowered and engaged. This empowerment is linked to higher levels of innovativeness, commitment to the organization, and overall job satisfaction. However, empowerment isn't universally beneficial; it depends significantly on the individual's need for achievement and growth. Some employees may thrive under more autonomous conditions, while others might feel overwhelmed by the increased responsibility.

Job Design and Employee Motivation

The design of individual jobs within the organization plays a crucial role in influencing employee behavior. Jobs that are crafted to include a variety of skills, provide a complete piece of work, have significant impact, and offer autonomy and feedback contribute to higher job satisfaction and motivation. This approach aligns with the principles of job enrichment, which aims to enhance job content by adding meaningful tasks that increase an employee's accountability and growth opportunities. For example, allowing an employee to handle a project from start to finish increases their task identity and significance, boosting their engagement and satisfaction with their work.

The Role of Networked Teams

Modern organizations often employ a networked approach, where cross-functional teams are formed to tackle specific projects or problems. This structure supports dynamic collaboration and leverages diverse skill sets, leading to innovative solutions and products. However, managing such teams requires clear communication channels and well-defined roles to prevent confusion and overlap of responsibilities. The success of networked teams hinges on the organization's ability to manage these complexities effectively.

Communication Flows

Organizational design also dictates the flow of communication within the company. Structures with many layers of management might slow down communication and make the organization less responsive to changes. On the other hand, organizations with minimal layers can facilitate quicker communication and faster decision-making but may suffer from a lack of clarity in roles and responsibilities if not managed carefully.

Cultural Impact

The organizational structure can reinforce or undermine the company culture. For instance, a hierarchical structure might support a culture of order and authority, while a more decentralized structure might promote a culture of innovation and flexibility. The alignment of structure with organizational culture is critical as it affects how employees perceive their roles and their alignment with the company's values and objectives.

Managing Change in Organizational Design

Changes in organizational design can have profound psychological impacts on employees, affecting their sense of security and their engagement with their work. Managing these changes effectively requires transparent communication about the reasons for the change, the benefits it brings, and how it will be implemented. Involving employees in the change process can help mitigate resistance and increase buy-in.

Organizational design is a powerful determinant of employee behavior. It shapes the way work is performed and influences employees' attitudes towards their jobs and the organization. Effective organizational design aligns the structure of the company with its strategic objectives while also catering to the needs of its employees, thereby enhancing productivity and satisfaction.

Creating and Managing Organizational Culture

Organizational culture is a complex framework of shared values, beliefs, and practices that shapes how work gets done within an organization. It significantly influences employee behavior, engagement, and performance. Creating and managing an effective organizational culture requires deliberate actions and strategies to align the culture with the organization's goals and values.

Defining and Communicating Core Values

The first step in shaping organizational culture is to clearly define and communicate the core values. These values should reflect the essence of the organization's identity and serve as a compass for behavior and decision-making within the company. It is crucial that these values are not just stated but are made visible through daily actions and decisions. This helps in creating a culture where values are lived and breathed, rather than being just words on a page.

Leadership and Role Modeling

Leaders play a pivotal role in setting the cultural tone of the organization. Their behavior and the consistency between their actions and the organization's values are critical in cultivating the desired culture. Leaders must embody the core values and demonstrate them through their actions. For example, if a company values transparency and open communication, leaders should practice this by being accessible and open to feedback, and by communicating important decisions and the reasons behind them transparently.

Employee Involvement and Engagement

Involving employees at all levels in the dialogue about culture helps in assessing the pulse of the current culture and in identifying areas for improvement. This can be achieved through surveys, focus groups, and open forums that allow employees to voice their opinions and suggestions. Engaging employees in this way not only helps in making them feel valued but also ensures that the culture evolves in a way that supports the needs and well-being of everyone in the organization.

Aligning HR Practices

Human Resources plays a crucial role in reinforcing organizational culture through various practices. This includes recruitment processes that screen for cultural fit, onboarding programs that introduce new hires to the company culture, performance management systems that reward behaviors aligned with the company values, and training and development programs that promote required skills and competencies. For instance, if teamwork and collaboration are valued, HR should implement team-building activities and collaboration tools that facilitate these practices.

Celebrating and Reinforcing Cultural Artifacts

Organizational culture is often expressed through artifacts such as rituals, ceremonies, and symbols. For example, recognizing and rewarding employees not just for outstanding performance but for embodying core values reinforces those values and encourages others to emulate them. Celebratory events, recognition programs, and even the physical layout of the workplace can serve as reflections of organizational culture and help in strengthening it.

Continuous Assessment and Adaptation

Culture is dynamic, not static. It needs to be continuously assessed and adapted as the organization evolves and as external conditions change. Regularly revisiting and reassessing the culture to ensure it remains relevant and aligned with the organization's goals is crucial. This might involve periodic reviews of cultural values, practices, and outcomes to determine what adjustments are needed to keep the culture vibrant and effective.

Managing Cultural Change

Changing an established culture can be challenging. It requires a clear vision of the desired culture, strong leadership to drive the change, and effective communication to get buy-in from all levels of the organization. It is important to manage the transition carefully by addressing concerns, providing clear reasons for the change, and outlining the benefits to both the organization and its employees.

Creating and managing organizational culture is a strategic process that requires commitment and consistency. It is about crafting a work environment that fosters the right behaviors and practices aligned with the organization's goals. As Peter Drucker famously said, "Culture eats strategy for breakfast," underscoring the importance of culture in achieving organizational success. By actively shaping and nurturing the culture, organizations can create a strong foundation that supports long-term success and employee satisfaction.

Psychological Impact of Organizational Change and How to Manage It

Organizational change is an inevitable aspect of modern business environments, driven by factors such as technological advancements, market dynamics, and shifts in consumer preferences. While change can lead to positive outcomes like improved efficiency and competitiveness, it often has a profound psychological impact on employees. Understanding and managing these effects is crucial for maintaining workforce stability and productivity.

Understanding the Psychological Impact

Stress and Anxiety: Changes in organizational structure, job roles, or business processes can create uncertainty and fear among employees. Concerns about job security, alterations in responsibilities, and the need to learn new skills can lead to increased stress and anxiety.

Resistance to Change: Psychological resistance is a common response to change. This resistance often stems from a natural human preference for stability and predictability. Employees might fear losing control over their work environment or doubt their ability to meet new expectations.

Sense of Loss: Organizational change can involve modifications to teams, management, or work roles that disrupt established relationships and routines. Employees may grieve the loss of their familiar work environment, colleagues, or previous roles, impacting their emotional well-being and productivity.

Cognitive Dissonance: When organizational changes conflict with employees' values or beliefs, it can lead to cognitive dissonance. This psychological discomfort arises when individuals find their beliefs are inconsistent with their actions, leading to stress and a potential decrease in job satisfaction.

Strategies for Managing Psychological Impacts

Effective Communication: Clear, transparent communication about the reasons for changes, expected outcomes, and the steps involved can help reduce uncertainty and alleviate anxiety. It is important for management to communicate not only the what and the how but also the why of changes, helping employees understand the necessity and benefits of the adjustments.

Participation and Empowerment: Involving employees in the change process can mitigate resistance and increase buy-in. When employees are part of decision-making processes, they are more likely to feel in control and less threatened by the change. This can be facilitated through workshops, brainstorming sessions, and feedback mechanisms that allow employees to contribute their ideas and express concerns.

Support Systems: Providing support through training and counseling can help employees adjust to change more effectively. Training programs should be designed to equip employees with the necessary skills to handle new systems or processes. Additionally, counseling services and stress management workshops can offer employees strategies to cope with change-related anxiety.

Acknowledging and Managing Emotions: Leaders should be trained to recognize and empathetically respond to the emotions and concerns of their employees. Acknowledging that feelings of loss or fear are valid and providing a supportive environment where employees can express these feelings can aid in the emotional adjustment process.

Gradual Implementation: Whenever possible, implementing changes gradually can help employees adjust better. Phased approaches allow employees to adapt to new systems or structures without feeling overwhelmed. This also provides the opportunity to make adjustments based on feedback, enhancing the overall effectiveness of the change process.

Celebrating Milestones: Recognizing and celebrating milestones during the change process can boost morale and reinforce the benefits of the change. Celebrations can be simple acknowledgments of completed training, successful implementation of a new system, or positive outcomes achieved because of the change.

The psychological impact of organizational change is significant and, if not managed properly, can lead to reduced employee morale and productivity. By employing thoughtful strategies that prioritize communication, participation, support, and emotional intelligence, organizations can not only reduce the negative impacts of change but also enhance employee engagement and loyalty. This holistic approach ensures that change is not just something to be endured but an opportunity for growth and improvement.

Part–IV

Applying Psychology to Management Practices

Chapter–9

Performance Management

"Performance Expectations = Results + Actions & Behaviors"

Understanding performance management involves delving into the psychological principles that underpin goal setting and expectations, the impact of feedback mechanisms, and the design of effective reward systems. Psychological principles play a crucial role in setting goals and expectations, encompassing attributes such as goal difficulty, specificity, acceptance, commitment, and feedback. These principles guide the formulation of goals that motivate and challenge employees, ultimately influencing their performance and job satisfaction. Feedback mechanisms, when effectively implemented, have significant psychological effects, providing employees with valuable insights into their performance, fostering motivation, and facilitating continuous improvement. Moreover, the design of effective reward systems is essential for recognizing and reinforcing desired behaviors and outcomes, aligning with the psychological need for acknowledgment and appreciation, and ultimately driving employee engagement and organizational success.

Psychological Principles in Setting Goals and Expectations

The process of setting goals and expectations within an organization is deeply rooted in psychological principles that influence employee motivation, engagement, and performance. Understanding these principles can greatly enhance the effectiveness of goal-setting practices.

Clarity and Specificity

Goals that are clear and specific provide employees with a distinct understanding of what is expected of them. This clarity reduces ambiguity, which can be a major source of stress in the workplace. Specific goals also allow for easier measurement of progress and performance, which is crucial for both feedback and adjustments along the way. The specificity of goals ensures that both managers and employees are aligned, which enhances the ability to focus efforts and resources efficiently.

Involvement and Ownership

When employees are involved in the goal-setting process, they are more likely to be committed to achieving those goals. This sense of ownership can be empowering as it gives employees a feeling of control over their work and its outcomes. Participatory goal setting encourages a deeper engagement with tasks, fostering an environment where employees are motivated to excel, not just comply.

Alignment with Personal and Organisational Values

Goals should not only align with the strategic objectives of the organization but also resonate with the personal values and aspirations of the employees. When employees see how their work contributes to larger organizational goals and aligns with their own values, they are more likely to find their work meaningful. This alignment enhances job satisfaction and can significantly boost motivation and loyalty.

Realistic and Challenging

Goals should strike a balance between being attainable and challenging. If goals are set too high, they can lead to frustration and demotivation due to the perceived unattainability. Conversely, goals that are too easy may not push employees to fully utilize their potential, leading to boredom or lack of fulfillment. Effective goals challenge employees to stretch their capabilities while still being realistically achievable.

Feedback Integration

Setting goals is just the beginning; providing ongoing feedback related to these goals is crucial for maintaining direction and motivation. Feedback helps employees understand how they are doing in relation to their goals and what adjustments may be necessary. Constructive feedback should be timely and specific, focusing on what can be improved and acknowledging what is working well.

Psychological Safety

Creating an environment where employees feel safe to take risks and possibly fail is crucial in a goal-oriented setting. Psychological safety allows employees to experiment and learn from their mistakes, which is essential for innovation and growth. When employees fear negative consequences for failure, they are less likely to pursue challenging goals or think creatively.

Continuous Learning and Adaptation

Goals should be dynamic and flexible, adapting to changes in the business environment or in employee capabilities and roles. Regular reviews of goals to reflect new information or priorities help keep the organization agile and responsive. This adaptability prevents goals from becoming obsolete or misaligned with the current context, ensuring that efforts are always directed towards relevant outcomes.

The psychological principles underlying goal setting are fundamental to crafting strategies that not only propel the organization towards its objectives but also enhance employee well-being and development. As Edwin Locke and Gary Latham, pioneers of goal-setting theory, suggest, goals are not just endpoints but are crucial drivers of motivation and performance. By integrating these psychological insights into goal-setting practices, organizations can foster a motivated, engaged, and high-performing workforce.

Feedback Mechanisms and Their Psychological Effects

Feedback mechanisms are essential components of performance management, influencing not only the productivity and quality of work but also the psychological well-being and professional growth of employees. Understanding the psychological effects of feedback can help organizations design processes that enhance employee performance and satisfaction.

Types of Feedback

Feedback can be categorized into several types, each with distinct psychological impacts:

1. **Positive Feedback**: This involves affirming comments about past behaviours, meant to reinforce and encourage similar actions in the future. Psychologically, positive feedback increases motivation and boosts confidence, making it a powerful tool for promoting desired behaviours.
2. **Constructive Feedback**: Unlike criticism, constructive feedback is aimed at improvement. It focuses on specific behaviours rather than the person and includes suggestions for growth. This type of feedback is crucial for learning and development, though it requires a sensitive approach to avoid defensive reactions.
3. **Negative Feedback**: This points out undesired or problematic behaviours and outcomes. While necessary, it can lead to adverse psychological effects such as decreased job satisfaction and self-esteem if not handled carefully.
4. **Formative Feedback**: Given during the process of completing a task, formative feedback helps to shape the behaviour as it happens. It's particularly effective in educational and developmental settings, promoting learning and adjustment before tasks are completed.
5. **Summative Feedback**: This is typically provided at the end of a task or project to assess the final outcome. It helps in evaluating overall performance

but may not be as effective in promoting immediate behavioural changes compared to formative feedback.

Psychological Effects of Feedback

The way feedback is perceived and processed can significantly affect an employee's attitude and behaviour:

- **Motivation and Engagement**: Effective feedback can enhance motivation and engagement by making employees feel valued and involved. Positive and constructive feedback helps individuals understand that their efforts are recognized and that they have a clear path for growth and improvement.
- **Stress and Anxiety**: Poorly delivered feedback can lead to stress and anxiety. Negative feedback, if not accompanied by support and guidance, can undermine confidence and increase job-related stress.
- **Learning and Development**: Feedback is a critical component of professional development. It can encourage continuous learning and adaptation by providing insights into performance and areas for improvement. Constructive feedback, in particular, is linked to higher levels of growth and development.
- **Relationship Dynamics**: Feedback can also influence relationships within the workplace. Transparent and respectful feedback fosters trust and respect between employees and management. Conversely, inconsistent or unfairly delivered feedback can lead to resentment and a breakdown in professional relationships.

Best Practices for Delivering Feedback

- **Timeliness**: Feedback should be given as close to the event as possible to ensure it is relevant and actionable.
- **Specificity**: Feedback should be specific and tied to observable behaviours rather than general traits. This specificity makes the feedback more actionable and less likely to be perceived as a personal attack.
- **Frequency**: Regular feedback is more effective than feedback given sporadically. Continuous feedback helps to create an ongoing dialogue about performance and development.
- **Balanced Approach**: While it's important to address areas for improvement, balancing this with positive feedback ensures that employees feel appreciated and valued, not just critiqued.
- **Two-Way Communication**: Feedback should not be a one-way street. Encouraging a dialogue where employees can express their perspectives and concerns makes the feedback process more interactive and less intimidating.

Feedback mechanisms, when designed and implemented thoughtfully, can have profound positive impacts on an organization. They enhance not only performance but also job satisfaction and employee retention by fostering an environment of continuous improvement and open communication.

Designing Effective Reward Systems

Reward systems are crucial in motivating employees, reinforcing desired behaviours, and aligning individual performances with organizational goals. An effective reward system should be comprehensive, fair, and adaptable to the changing needs of the organization and its workforce.

Foundations of Reward Systems

1. **Alignment with Organizational Objectives**: Rewards should be directly linked to key performance indicators and organizational objectives. This alignment ensures that the rewards drive behaviours that contribute to the organization's success, making the system both relevant and strategic.
2. **Equity and Fairness**: The perception of fairness is critical. Rewards must be distributed based on clear and measurable performance criteria to avoid biases and favouritism. Ensuring that all employees understand how rewards are determined can enhance the system's credibility and effectiveness.
3. **Diversity of Rewards**: Incorporating a variety of rewards can cater to the different needs and preferences of employees. While monetary rewards are common, non-monetary rewards such as public recognition, career development opportunities, and flexible working conditions can also be highly motivating.

Types of Rewards

1. **Monetary Rewards**: These include salaries, bonuses, and profit-sharing schemes. Monetary rewards are powerful but need to be structured carefully to ensure they are sustainable and perceived as fair.

2. **Non-Monetary Rewards**: Examples include professional development opportunities, awards, additional leave, and flexible work arrangements. These rewards can enhance job satisfaction and loyalty without the direct costs associated with monetary rewards.

3. **Performance-Based Rewards**: These are tied directly to individual or team performance metrics. Performance-based rewards not only motivate high performance but also provide clear benchmarks for success.

4. **Recognition Programs**: Formal and informal recognition can significantly boost morale and motivation. Recognition programs might include employee of the month awards, commendations in company communications, or informal acknowledgements in meetings.

Psychological Impacts of Reward Systems

1. **Motivation**: Effective reward systems boost motivation by providing clear incentives and recognising achievements. Both intrinsic and extrinsic motivations are important; while extrinsic rewards (like bonuses) provide immediate gratification, intrinsic rewards (like personal growth) offer long-term satisfaction.

2. **Employee Retention**: Well-designed reward systems can improve employee retention by creating a positive work environment and demonstrating that the organization values its employees.

3. **Cultural Reinforcement**: Rewards can reinforce the desired organizational culture by promoting

behaviours that align with the organization's values and objectives.

Challenges in Reward System Design

1. **Maintaining Relevance**: Organizations must continually assess and update their reward systems to ensure they remain relevant to both the employees and the organization. This includes staying competitive in the market and adapting to changes in the workforce.
2. **Balancing Cost and Impact**: Designing reward systems that are cost-effective yet impactful is a significant challenge. It requires strategic planning and creativity to maximize the benefits while managing costs.
3. **Avoiding Unintended Consequences**: Poorly designed reward systems can lead to unintended consequences such as unhealthy competition, a focus on short-term gains over long-term objectives, or manipulation of the system.

Implementing Reward Systems

1. **Communication**: Clear communication about how the reward system works, the criteria for rewards, and the way rewards relate to performance is essential. Transparency in the process builds trust and understanding.
2. **Feedback and Adaptation**: Regular feedback from employees can help identify issues and areas for improvement in the reward system. An adaptable approach allows the organization to make necessary adjustments to enhance the system's effectiveness and fairness.

3. **Integration with Other HR Systems**: Reward systems should be integrated with other HR processes like performance management, training, and development. This integration ensures a holistic approach to employee management and development.

Effective reward systems are vital for motivating employees, enhancing performance, and achieving organizational goals. They require careful design and management to ensure they are fair, effective, and aligned with the strategic objectives of the organization. By considering the diverse needs of their workforce and the strategic goals of the organization, HR managers can craft reward systems that not only motivate but also foster a positive and productive work environment.

Chapter–10

Stress, Well-being, and Coping Mechanisms

Understanding stress, well-being, and coping mechanisms is essential for promoting mental health and managing workplace stress. The psychological impact of workplace stress can lead to physical and psychological distress, affecting both employees' well-being and organizational productivity. Promoting mental health in the workplace involves creating a supportive environment that addresses stressors and provides resources for employees to maintain their well-being. Coping strategies for managers and their teams are crucial for mitigating the effects of stress. Open communication, access to mental health resources, and fostering a culture of support and understanding are vital components of promoting mental well-being in the workplace.

Understanding and Managing Workplace Stress

Workplace stress is a significant concern for both employees and employers, impacting not only individual health but also organizational productivity and morale. Effective management of workplace stress requires a comprehensive approach that addresses both the sources of stress and the strategies individuals can use to cope with it.

Identification of Stressors

The first step in managing workplace stress is to identify the specific stressors. These can vary widely depending on the type of work, the organizational environment, and individual perceptions. Common stressors include high workload, unclear job expectations, lack of control over work activities, and interpersonal conflicts. Conducting regular assessments such as surveys and focus groups can help organizations identify these stressors and understand their impact on employees.

Organizational Strategies to Reduce Stress

1. **Job Redesign**: Modifying job roles to ensure that they are clear and achievable can help reduce stress. This might involve clarifying job responsibilities, providing the necessary resources, or adjusting workloads to ensure they are manageable.

2. **Improving Organizational Communication**: Effective communication can alleviate many uncertainties contributing to workplace stress. Keeping employees informed about organizational changes, providing clear instructions, and opening channels for employees to voice concerns can create a more transparent and less stressful work environment.

3. **Promoting Work-Life Balance**: Encouraging employees to maintain a balance between their work and personal life is crucial. This can be facilitated

by offering flexible working arrangements, such as telecommuting options and flexible hours, and by ensuring that employees are not consistently overburdened with excessive overtime.

4. **Support Systems**: Providing access to support services such as Employee Assistance Programs (EAPs) can help employees manage stress more effectively. These programs offer a range of services, including counseling, which can assist employees in dealing with both work-related and personal stressors.

Individual Coping Strategies

1. **Time Management**: Effective time management can help reduce job stress by enabling employees to handle their duties within a manageable schedule. Techniques include prioritizing tasks, breaking projects into smaller steps, and delegating when appropriate.
2. **Development of Interpersonal Skills**: Enhancing skills such as communication and conflict resolution can help employees manage and reduce stress arising from interpersonal issues at work.
3. **Relaxation Techniques**: Employees can benefit from techniques such as deep breathing, meditation, or yoga, which help reduce the physical and psychological symptoms of stress. Encouraging regular breaks and physical activities can also help alleviate stress.
4. **Professional Development**: Continuous learning and skill development can help employees feel more

competent and confident in their roles, which can reduce stress levels. Providing opportunities for professional growth can also help employees feel more valued and supported by the organization.

Creating a Supportive Work Environment

1. **Leadership Training**: Training managers to recognize signs of stress among their teams is vital. Effective leaders can help mitigate stress by providing support, facilitating fair workloads, and creating an open environment where employees feel comfortable discussing their stressors.

2. **Fostering a Positive Work Culture**: A workplace culture that promotes mutual respect, recognition, and constructive feedback can significantly reduce stress levels. Cultivating a positive environment where employees feel safe and valued is essential for reducing workplace stress.

3. **Regular Review and Adaptation**: Organizations should regularly review their stress management strategies to ensure they remain effective and relevant. This includes seeking feedback from employees on the effectiveness of current strategies and making adjustments as necessary.

Managing workplace stress effectively requires a proactive approach that combines organizational changes with support for individual coping strategies. By addressing both the sources of stress and providing tools for managing it, organizations can create healthier, more productive workplaces.

Promoting Mental Health in the Workplace

Promoting mental health in the workplace is crucial for maintaining a productive, healthy, and engaged workforce. It involves creating an environment that supports psychological well-being and addresses mental health issues proactively. This commitment to mental health can lead to reduced absenteeism, enhanced morale, and increased productivity.

Development of Mental Health Policies

1. **Comprehensive Mental Health Strategies**: Organizations should develop clear, comprehensive mental health policies that outline their commitment to promoting mental well-being. These policies should include prevention, early intervention, support for recovery, and continuous promotion of mental health awareness.

2. **Anti-Stigma Campaigns**: A significant barrier to mental health support in the workplace is stigma. Implementing campaigns that educate and change negative attitudes towards mental illness can encourage a more open and supportive environment for discussing and addressing mental health issues.

Training and Resources

1. **Mental Health Training for Managers**: Training leaders and managers to recognize signs of mental distress and understand mental health issues is critical. Equipped with this knowledge, managers can provide appropriate support to their teams and guide them towards available resources.

2. **Employee Education**: Regular workshops and

seminars about mental health can raise awareness among all employees. Topics might include stress management, the importance of mental health, how to seek help, and ways to support colleagues who are facing mental health challenges.

3. **Access to Professional Help**: Providing employees with access to mental health professionals such as psychologists or licensed therapists through Employee Assistance Programs (EAPs) or health benefits plans can promote mental well-being. These services should be confidential to encourage utilization without fear of judgment or repercussions.

Supportive Workplace Environment

1. **Flexible Work Arrangements**: Flexibility in work arrangements can significantly reduce stress and improve mental health. Options like telecommuting, flexible hours, and part-time work can help employees balance work with personal life demands.

2. **Work-Life Balance Initiatives**: Beyond flexible work hours, initiatives that promote a healthy work-life balance are essential. This could include setting clear boundaries around work hours, encouraging regular breaks, and supporting leisure and social activities outside of work.

3. **Peer Support Programs**: Establishing peer support systems where employees can share their experiences and support each other can be very beneficial. These programs provide a sense of community and belonging, reducing feelings of isolation and stress.

Monitoring and Continuous Improvement

1. **Regular Assessment of Mental Health Initiatives**: To ensure the effectiveness of mental health strategies, organizations should regularly assess their impact. This can be done through employee surveys, feedback sessions, and reviewing usage data of mental health services.
2. **Adaptation of Strategies**: Based on the assessments, strategies may need to be adapted to meet the changing needs of the workforce or to address areas where current initiatives are not effective. Continuous improvement will help organizations stay responsive to their employees' mental health needs.

Promoting mental health in the workplace is an ongoing process that requires dedicated effort from all levels of the organization. By implementing robust policies, providing necessary training and resources, fostering a supportive work environment, and committing to continuous assessment and improvement, organizations can create a workplace where mental health is prioritized and supported.

Coping Strategies for Managers and Their Teams

Effective coping strategies are essential for managers and their teams to handle the stresses and challenges of the workplace. These strategies not only help in managing current stressors but also in building resilience against future challenges.

For Managers

1. **Emotional Intelligence**: Managers should cultivate emotional intelligence, which involves being aware of, controlling, and expressing one's emotions healthily and empathetically. Emotional intelligence helps managers handle interpersonal relationships judiciously and empathetically, an essential skill in stressful situations.
2. **Delegation**: Effective delegation is not just a time management tool but also a stress reduction strategy. By delegating tasks appropriately, managers can reduce their workload and stress levels while empowering their team members and aiding their development.
3. **Prioritization and Time Management**: Managers should master prioritization and time management techniques to cope with high workloads and tight deadlines. Tools like Eisenhower Box (urgent-important matrix) can help in prioritizing tasks effectively.
4. **Communication Skills**: Open and transparent communication can prevent misunderstandings and conflicts in the team that might lead to stress. Regular meetings and feedback sessions help ensure that everyone is on the same page and can voice their concerns or suggestions.
5. **Self-care**: Managers often prioritize the needs of their teams and neglect their own. Engaging in regular physical activity, maintaining a healthy diet, getting sufficient sleep, and pursuing hobbies can help managers maintain their mental and physical health.

For Teams

1. **Stress Awareness and Management Training**: Providing teams with training in recognizing signs of stress and managing it can be very beneficial. Techniques such as mindfulness, meditation, and stress management workshops can equip team members with the tools they need to handle stress effectively.
2. **Team Building Activities**: Regular team-building activities can improve relationships and communication within the team, leading to a more supportive environment. These activities can also offer a break from routine work, providing a refreshing change.
3. **Supportive Environment**: Creating a culture where team members feel safe to express their concerns and ask for help when needed is crucial. This could be facilitated by regular check-ins and creating an open-door policy where team members feel comfortable approaching their managers with issues.
4. **Conflict Resolution Mechanisms**: Implementing effective conflict resolution mechanisms within the team can prevent conflicts from escalating and causing stress. Training in conflict resolution and encouraging a culture of respect and understanding are key.
5. **Recognition and Rewards**: Recognizing and rewarding the hard work and achievements of team members can boost morale and reduce stress. This recognition can be as simple as a public

acknowledgment in a team meeting or more formal rewards like bonuses or extra days off.

Cross-Cutting Strategies

1. **Flexible Work Options**: Both managers and teams can benefit from flexible work options, such as remote working or flexible hours. These arrangements can help individuals manage their work and personal life more effectively, reducing stress.
2. **Resource Accessibility**: Ensuring that both managers and their teams have access to necessary resources, whether these are tools, information, or personnel, can reduce frustration and stress caused by resource shortages.
3. **Mental Health Resources**: Providing access to mental health resources, such as counselling services or mental health days, supports the overall well-being of both managers and their teams.

Coping strategies for stress in the workplace are vital for maintaining a healthy work environment and ensuring the well-being of both managers and their teams. By implementing these strategies, organizations can enhance their team's resilience, improve productivity, and reduce the likelihood of burnout. Effective coping mechanisms tailored to both individual and team needs are essential components of a successful organizational strategy.

Chapter–11

Innovation and Creativity

Understanding the psychological drivers of innovation and creativity is crucial for fostering a culture of continuous improvement and original thinking within organizations. Psychological research emphasizes the significance of intrinsic motivation, autonomy, and a supportive environment in stimulating creativity and innovation. By recognizing and leveraging these drivers, organizations can cultivate an environment that encourages experimentation, risk-taking, and the exploration of novel ideas. Fostering an innovative culture involves creating an atmosphere that values diverse perspectives, encourages open communication, and embraces calculated risk-taking. Moreover, managing creative teams and processes requires a balance between providing structure and autonomy, facilitating collaboration, and recognizing and rewarding innovative contributions. By understanding the psychological underpinnings of creativity and innovation, organizations can create an environment that nurtures and harnesses the potential of their employees' creative abilities.

Psychological Drivers of Innovation and Creativity

Innovation and creativity are not merely about generating new ideas; they are about transforming these ideas into practical and novel solutions that can drive organizational success. Understanding the psychological underpinnings of these processes is crucial for fostering an environment where creativity thrives.

Intrinsic Motivation

Intrinsic motivation is a key driver of creativity. When individuals engage in tasks that they find personally rewarding, they are more likely to be creative. This type of motivation enhances engagement and persistence, which are critical for the creative process. As Teresa Amabile suggests, the freedom to explore ideas and the joy derived from the task itself can significantly boost creative outputs.

Cognitive Flexibility

Cognitive flexibility refers to the ability to switch between different concepts or to think about multiple concepts simultaneously. This flexibility allows individuals to see problems from various angles and to come up with innovative solutions. Training in creative problem-solving techniques can enhance this cognitive flexibility, leading to more innovative outcomes.

Risk Tolerance

Innovation inherently involves risk as it requires venturing into the unknown. A culture that supports risk-taking and views failures as learning opportunities is essential for fostering creativity. Organizations that celebrate small wins and constructive failures encourage their employees to take risks, which is a critical component of the creative process.

Openness to Experience

Psychological research has consistently linked openness to experience—one of the five major personality traits—with creativity. Individuals who score high on this trait tend to have a broad range of interests, prefer variety over routine, and are more receptive to new experiences. Encouraging employees to step outside their comfort zones and exposing them to different perspectives can stimulate creative thinking.

Environmental Influence

The work environment can significantly impact creativity. Spaces that encourage interaction and provide a stimulating atmosphere can enhance creative output. Elements such as flexible workspaces, access to resources, and a supportive atmosphere play crucial roles in nurturing an innovative mindset.

Social Dynamics

Creativity does not occur in isolation; it often thrives in collaborative settings where ideas can be shared and refined. The dynamics within a team, including how members interact and share knowledge, can significantly influence the creative process. Facilitating effective communication and collaboration within teams is therefore essential for fostering innovation.

Psychological Safety

A key element in fostering a creative organizational culture is psychological safety. This concept involves creating an environment where employees feel safe to express their ideas without fear of ridicule or punishment. When team members feel secure, they are more likely to share their innovative ideas and contribute to the creative process.

Leadership Influence

Leaders play a pivotal role in driving innovation by setting the tone for the organization's culture. Leaders who encourage experimentation and support creative efforts inspire their teams to pursue innovative solutions. Effective leaders also know how to balance the need for creativity with the organization's strategic objectives, ensuring that creative efforts align with business goals. Understanding these psychological drivers provides a foundation for developing strategies that enhance creativity and innovation within an organization. By fostering an environment that supports these drivers, organizations can enhance their capacity for innovation and maintain a competitive edge in the marketplace.

Fostering an Innovative Culture

Creating a culture that consistently fosters innovation involves more than just encouraging employees to come up with new ideas; it requires a holistic approach that permeates the entire organizational structure and influences its core practices and policies.

Leadership Commitment to Innovation

The role of leadership in fostering an innovative culture cannot be overstated. Leaders must not only advocate for innovation but also demonstrate it through their actions and decisions. This includes providing the necessary resources for innovation initiatives and actively participating in the innovation process. Leaders should set a clear vision for innovation that aligns with the organization's strategic goals and communicate this vision effectively to all levels of the organization.

Cultivating an Open and Inclusive Environment

An innovative culture thrives in an environment where all employees feel they can contribute ideas and that their contributions are valued. Creating a space that values diversity in thought, background, and experience can lead to a richer pool of ideas and perspectives, driving more effective innovation. This involves implementing policies that promote diversity and inclusion and actively working to eliminate any biases that might stifle creativity.

Psychological Safety

A foundational element of an innovative culture is psychological safety, where employees feel safe to take risks and express their ideas without fear of negative consequences. This sense of security encourages experimentation and can lead to breakthrough innovations. Organizations should strive to create an atmosphere where failures are seen as a natural part of the learning process and where constructive feedback is given to help employees learn and grow from their experiences.

Encouraging Collaboration and Communication

Innovation often comes from the cross-pollination of ideas between different areas of an organization. Facilitating collaboration across departments and teams can help break down silos and encourage a more holistic approach to innovation. This might involve creating mixed teams for projects, organizing regular cross-departmental meetings, and using collaborative technologies that enhance communication across the organization.

Continuous Learning and Adaptability

For a culture of innovation to thrive, an organization must commit to continuous learning and adaptability. This means not only keeping up with industry trends and technological advancements but also continuously evaluating and adapting internal processes and strategies to support innovation. Providing employees with opportunities for professional development and learning can also keep them engaged and motivated to contribute to the organization's innovative efforts.

Recognition and Rewards

Recognizing and rewarding innovative efforts is crucial in reinforcing a culture of innovation. This doesn't only apply to successful outcomes but also to the willingness to innovate and take risks. Reward systems should be designed to acknowledge various forms of innovation, from incremental improvements to major breakthroughs, ensuring that employees feel appreciated for their creative efforts.

Structured Yet Flexible Innovation Processes

While creativity often requires freedom, having structured processes for managing innovation can ensure that ideas are effectively captured, evaluated, and implemented. This includes having clear criteria for selecting which ideas to develop, as well as defined pathways for turning these ideas into actionable projects. However, it's important that these processes remain flexible enough to adapt to new information and circumstances. Fostering an innovative culture is a dynamic and ongoing process that requires attention and effort across all levels of an organization. By committing to these principles, organizations can create an environment where innovation is not just an occasional success but a continuous and integral part of the organizational fabric.

Managing Creative Teams and Processes

Managing creative teams and processes is a complex task that requires a nuanced understanding of both the creative process and the dynamics of team interaction. Effective management in this context not only supports the generation of innovative ideas but also ensures these ideas are executable and aligned with organizational goals.

Establishing a Vision and Objectives

1. **Clear Vision**: Leaders of creative teams need to establish and communicate a clear vision that aligns with the organization's broader objectives. This vision should inspire and provide a clear direction for the creative efforts of the team.

2. **Specific Objectives**: Alongside a broad vision, specific, measurable objectives should be set to guide the creative process and provide criteria against which to evaluate creative outputs. These objectives can help maintain focus and drive efforts towards tangible outcomes.

Cultivating the Right Team Dynamics

1. **Diverse Teams**: Creativity thrives in environments where diverse perspectives are available. Assembling teams with varied backgrounds, skills, and cognitive styles can enhance problem-solving capabilities and lead to more innovative solutions.
2. **Team Roles**: Clearly defined roles within the creative team help ensure that all necessary functions are covered and that team members understand their responsibilities and how they contribute to the team's objectives.
3. **Communication Norms**: Establishing norms for open and respectful communication encourages team members to express their ideas and feedback without fear of dismissal or ridicule, fostering a more collaborative and innovative team environment.

Facilitating the Creative Process

1. **Idea Generation**: Techniques such as brainstorming, mind mapping, or SCAMPER can facilitate the generation of new ideas. It's crucial that during these sessions, all ideas are welcomed, and judgment is reserved to encourage uninhibited creative thinking.
2. **Prototyping and Experimentation**: Encouraging rapid prototyping and experimentation can help teams quickly test the feasibility of their ideas and learn from failures without significant resource expenditure.
3. **Feedback Loops**: Regular and constructive feedback is essential in guiding the creative process

and refining ideas. Feedback should be timely, specific, and focused on the idea rather than the individual, to encourage growth and improvement.

Managing Workflow and Resources

1. **Resource Allocation**: Adequate resources, whether time, budget, or tools, need to be allocated to support the creative processes. Managers need to ensure that teams have what they need to execute their ideas effectively.

2. **Workflow Management**: Balancing structure and flexibility is key in managing creative workflows. While some structure is necessary to ensure productivity and alignment with goals, too much can stifle creativity. Adaptive project management methodologies like Agile can be particularly effective in creative projects.

3. **Time Management**: Creative work can often be non-linear and unpredictable. Managers should ensure that timelines are flexible enough to allow for creativity while still maintaining enough structure to meet deadlines.

Nurturing Creativity and Innovation

1. **Continuous Learning**: Encouraging continuous learning and development, both in individual craft and in broader skills such as creative thinking and problem-solving, helps keep team members sharp and engaged.

2. **Inspirational Inputs**: Exposing teams to a range of inspirational inputs, from industry trends and art to technology and science, can spark new ideas and approaches.

3. **Environment and Tools**: The physical and digital environments can significantly impact creativity. Spaces that are conducive to collaboration and concentration, equipped with the right tools and technologies, can enhance creative output.

Managing creative teams and processes effectively requires a balance of leadership, flexibility, and structured support. By strategically guiding teams, facilitating creativity, and managing resources and workflows effectively, managers can harness the full potential of their creative teams and drive innovation within their organizations.

Chapter–12

Future Trends and Challenges

Understanding the future of work and its psychological implications is crucial as organizations navigate the impact of remote and hybrid work models, technological advancements, and the preparation for future psychological challenges in management. The shift to remote and hybrid work models has significant implications for employees' psychological well-being, as it can affect their sense of connection, work-life balance, and mental health. Organizations need to proactively address these challenges by fostering a supportive virtual work environment, promoting social connections, and providing resources for managing stress and maintaining well-being. Additionally, technological advancements, such as automation and artificial intelligence, bring management implications related to job roles, skill development, and the psychological impact of change. Leaders must consider the psychological effects of these advancements on employees, including concerns about job security, skill relevance, and the need for reskilling and upskilling initiatives. Moreover, preparing for future psychological challenges in management involves anticipating the evolving needs of employees, such as addressing burnout, maintaining motivation, and supporting mental health in the face of ongoing changes in work dynamics and organizational structures.

The Impact of Remote and Hybrid Work Models on Psychological Well-Being

The shift towards remote and hybrid work models, accelerated by the COVID-19 pandemic, has brought significant changes to the traditional workplace dynamics. These changes have profound implications for the psychological well-being of employees, influencing everything from work-life balance to social interactions and mental health.

Work-Life Balance

Remote and hybrid work models offer the potential for a better work-life balance, a critical factor in employee well-being. The elimination of commuting time gives employees more flexibility to manage personal responsibilities alongside work. However, this flexibility can also blur the boundaries between work and home life, leading to extended work hours and difficulty in disengaging from work responsibilities. The challenge for organizations is to encourage clear boundaries that help employees manage this balance effectively.

Social Interaction and Isolation

One of the most significant impacts of remote work is on social interactions. While traditional office environments naturally foster incidental and planned social interactions, remote and hybrid models often reduce these opportunities, potentially leading to feelings of isolation and loneliness. This lack of social interaction can affect team cohesion and individual mental health, highlighting the need for organizations to find new ways to facilitate social connections among remote and hybrid employees.

Autonomy and Empowerment

Remote work inherently increases autonomy, allowing employees more control over their work environment and methods. This can lead to increased job satisfaction and empowerment. However, with greater autonomy also comes the need for strong self-discipline and management skills, which not all employees may possess. Organizations need to support employees in developing these skills and provide them with the tools to manage their new levels of autonomy effectively.

Mental Health Considerations

The psychological impact of remote and hybrid work can also manifest in increased stress, anxiety, and depression. The reasons vary from isolation and overwork to the stress of managing home life alongside work responsibilities. Employers must recognize these challenges and enhance their mental health support structures, ensuring employees have access to mental health resources and support systems.

Equity and Inclusion

Hybrid models, in particular, pose unique challenges for equity and inclusion. There is a risk of creating two distinct classes of employees—those who are seen and those who are unseen—depending on their physical presence in the office. This can affect promotions, project opportunities, and overall visibility within the company. To counteract this, organizations must be deliberate in their efforts to ensure all employees, regardless of their work location, are given equal opportunities and visibility.

Organizational Culture

Maintaining a cohesive organizational culture is another challenge in remote and hybrid models. The shared sense of purpose and community that is often built through in-person interactions needs to be deliberately cultivated through virtual means. Organizations must rethink their cultural activities and communication strategies to ensure they resonate and reach all employees effectively.

Technological Adaptation

The successful implementation of remote and hybrid work models heavily relies on technology. From communication tools to project management software, the ability to work effectively from various locations depends on robust technological infrastructure and ongoing support. Organizations must invest in the right tools and ensure all employees are trained to use them effectively. In conclusion, the shift to remote and hybrid work models has a multifaceted impact on the psychological well-being of employees. Organizations need to be proactive in addressing these impacts by implementing supportive policies, investing in technology, and fostering an inclusive and flexible work environment. This approach will not only help in managing the current challenges but also pave the way for a more resilient and adaptive workforce in the future.

Technological Advancements and Their Management Implications

As organizations navigate the evolving landscape of technological advancements, management practices must adapt to leverage these changes effectively while addressing the associated challenges. The implications of these advancements are profound, affecting every aspect of organizational operations and strategy.

Integration of Advanced Technologies

1. **Automation and Artificial Intelligence**: The integration of automation and AI into business processes is transforming industries by enhancing efficiency and enabling data-driven decision-making. However, this shift requires managers to rethink job roles and workflows, potentially leading to workforce displacement or the need for significant retraining.

2. **Internet of Things (IoT)**: IoT technology connects physical devices to the internet, facilitating more efficient operations and improved data collection. Managers must ensure robust security measures are in place to protect sensitive data and maintain the integrity of interconnected systems.

3. **Advanced Analytics and Big Data**: The ability to analyze vast amounts of data offers unprecedented insights into customer behavior, operational efficiency, and strategic opportunities. Managers need to cultivate a culture that can harness these insights effectively, ensuring that decision-making is informed by data rather than intuition.

Workforce and Workplace Transformation

1. **Remote Work Technologies**: As remote work becomes more prevalent, organizations must invest in technologies that support collaboration and communication across distributed teams. This includes virtual meeting tools, project management software, and secure access to corporate networks.
2. **Digital Skills and Literacy**: The rapid pace of technological change necessitates a workforce that is agile and able to continuously develop new skills. Managers face the challenge of driving ongoing education and training initiatives to keep their teams competent and competitive.
3. **Employee Monitoring and Privacy**: With the rise of remote work and digital tools, organizations have greater capacity to monitor employee activities. Managers must balance productivity monitoring with respect for privacy, ensuring that surveillance does not erode trust or employee morale.

Ethical and Social Implications

1. **Ethical AI Use**: As AI systems become more critical in decision-making processes, ensuring these systems are transparent and free from biases is essential. Managers must oversee the ethical deployment of AI, including the auditing of algorithms for fairness and accuracy.
2. **Technological Unemployment**: Automation and AI can lead to job displacement, raising ethical questions about the role of organizations in supporting affected employees. Managers must

consider strategies for reskilling employees and possibly reshaping business models to create new opportunities for human workers.

3. **Sustainability**: Technological advancements can also drive sustainability initiatives, such as energy-efficient processes and waste reduction. Managers are tasked with integrating sustainability into the core strategy, aligning technological investments with environmental goals.

Strategic Implications

1. **Innovation Management**: Keeping pace with technological change requires a strategic approach to innovation. Managers need to foster an environment where experimentation is encouraged, and innovative ideas can be tested and implemented quickly.
2. **Competitive Advantage**: Technology can be a significant source of competitive advantage, but only if it is aligned with the organization's strategic goals. Managers must ensure that technology investments enhance core competencies and deliver value to customers.
3. **Change Management**: Implementing new technologies often requires significant changes in organizational structure and processes. Effective change management practices are crucial to ensure a smooth transition and to maximize the benefits of new technologies.

As technological advancements continue to reshape the business landscape, the role of management becomes increasingly complex and critical. Managers must not only keep abreast of current technological trends but also anticipate future developments and prepare their organizations to adapt and thrive in an ever-changing environment.

Preparing for Future Psychological Challenges in Management

As organizations evolve and adapt to new technologies, work models, and global challenges, management must also prepare for the psychological impacts these changes have on the workforce. Anticipating and addressing these challenges proactively is crucial to maintaining a resilient and productive organization.

Enhancing Mental Health Support

1. **Comprehensive Mental Health Programs**: Organizations must expand their mental health support systems to include proactive measures such as regular mental health assessments, training for managers to recognize signs of mental distress, and access to professional mental health services.
2. **Stress Management Initiatives**: Implementing programs that help employees manage stress effectively, such as mindfulness training, stress management workshops, and relaxation spaces, can prevent mental health issues from escalating.
3. **Building Resilience**: Developing resilience training programs can equip employees to handle stress and adapt to change more effectively. These programs should focus on building emotional strength,

improving recovery from setbacks, and fostering a growth mindset.

Adapting to the Changing Nature of Work

1. **Remote and Hybrid Work Challenges**: As remote and hybrid work models become more common, managers need to find ways to support the psychological well-being of remote employees, which includes ensuring they feel connected and engaged with the broader team.

2. **Managing Work-Life Boundaries**: Providing guidance and tools to help employees manage the blurring lines between work and home life is essential. This might include training on setting boundaries, time management, and the use of digital tools to separate work from personal life.

3. **Cultural Sensitivity and Inclusion**: Global and diverse work settings require managers to be culturally sensitive and inclusive. Training programs that enhance understanding and respect for different cultures and backgrounds can help mitigate conflicts and enhance team cohesion.

Leveraging Technology Responsibly

1. **Ethical Use of Monitoring Tools**: While technology can help in monitoring productivity and well-being, it is crucial to use these tools ethically and transparently to avoid trust erosion. Clear policies should be established regarding what is monitored, why, and how the information is used.

2. **Addressing Technostress**: The constant influx of new technologies can lead to technostress, where

employees feel overwhelmed by keeping up with technological changes. Providing adequate training and support, and fostering an environment where it is okay to ask for help, can mitigate this stress.

3. **Digital Detox Initiatives**: Encouraging regular digital detoxes where employees take breaks from digital devices can help prevent burnout and promote better mental health and focus.

Fostering a Supportive Leadership Style

1. **Emotional Intelligence in Leadership**: Training leaders to recognize their own emotional states and those of their team members can improve management practices and lead to a more empathetic leadership style.
2. **Proactive Communication**: Cultivating a culture of open and proactive communication can alleviate uncertainties that may cause stress among employees. Regular updates, town hall meetings, and open Q&A sessions can help maintain clarity and reduce anxiety.
3. **Empowering Employees**: Providing employees with more control over their work and the way they achieve their goals can enhance job satisfaction and reduce psychological strain. This involves trust and a move away from micromanagement.

Preparing for future psychological challenges in management requires a multifaceted approach that combines proactive mental health support, adaptation to new work paradigms, responsible use of technology, and a supportive leadership style. By addressing these areas, managers can not only help their organizations navigate these challenges but also enhance the overall well-being and productivity of their workforce.

Appendix A: Case Studies

CS 1: Google's Project Aristotle

Topic: Team Dynamics

Description: In a quest to understand what makes some teams more effective than others, Google embarked on Project Aristotle in 2012. The goal was to determine the key dynamics that influence team success within their organization. After extensive research involving over 180 teams, Google identified five critical factors that contribute to effective teams: psychological safety, dependability, structure and clarity, meaning, and impact.

1. **Psychological Safety:** This was identified as the most crucial factor. Psychological safety refers to a team environment where individuals feel safe to take risks, express their thoughts and concerns, and be vulnerable without fear of negative consequences. Teams with high psychological safety tend to have members who are more willing to share ideas and take creative risks.

2. **Dependability:** Team members reliably complete quality work on time. Teams with high dependability trust each other to meet commitments and deliver results.

3. **Structure and Clarity:** Successful teams have clear roles, plans, and goals. Each member knows what is expected of them, which reduces ambiguity and increases efficiency.

4. **Meaning:** Team members find personal significance in their work. When individuals feel that their work is meaningful, they are more engaged and motivated.
5. **Impact:** Team members believe their work matters and creates change. Understanding the impact of their contributions enhances motivation and satisfaction.

Learning Outcome: Readers can draw valuable lessons from Google's findings to enhance team dynamics in their own professional and personal environments. Here are some practical steps to foster these key dynamics:

1. **Encouraging Psychological Safety:**
   - **Open Communication:** Create an environment where team members feel comfortable speaking up. Encourage sharing of ideas and feedback without fear of judgment.
   - **Showing Vulnerability:** Leaders can model vulnerability by admitting mistakes and asking for help. This sets a precedent that it's okay to be imperfect.
   - **Valuing Input:** Actively listen to each team member's contributions and acknowledge their ideas and efforts, reinforcing that everyone's voice matters.
2. **Building Dependability:**
   - **Set Clear Expectations:** Define roles and responsibilities clearly so that everyone knows what is expected of them.

- **Hold Accountable:** Establish regular check-ins to ensure commitments are being met and to address any obstacles promptly.

3. **Enhancing Structure and Clarity:**
   - **Define Goals:** Set specific, measurable, achievable, relevant, and time-bound (SMART) goals.
   - **Plan Strategically:** Develop clear plans and processes to achieve these goals, ensuring everyone understands the roadmap.
4. **Creating Meaning:**
   - **Align Work with Values:** Help team members connect their tasks with the larger mission of the organization.
   - **Recognize Contributions:** Highlight how individual efforts contribute to the team's success and the organization's goals.
5. **Ensuring Impact:**
   - **Share Success Stories:** Regularly communicate the impact of the team's work on the organization and its stakeholders.
   - **Celebrate Achievements:** Recognize and celebrate milestones and successes to reinforce the significance of the team's contributions.

By integrating these principles, readers can improve collaboration, trust, and overall team effectiveness, whether in a professional setting or personal relationships. Emphasizing psychological safety and the other dynamics identified by Project Aristotle can lead to more innovative, resilient, and successful teams.

CS 2: Apple's Leadership Transition from Steve Jobs to Tim Cook

Topic: Leadership Psychology

Description: The transition of leadership from Steve Jobs to Tim Cook at Apple marked a profound shift in the company's management style, providing a fascinating case study in leadership psychology. Steve Jobs, Apple's co-founder, was celebrated as a visionary leader whose autocratic and sometimes abrasive style drove the company to unprecedented heights of innovation and success. His approach was characterized by an intense focus on product perfection, a hands-on management style, and a relentless drive for high standards. Jobs' leadership was instrumental in the creation of groundbreaking products such as the iPhone, iPad, and MacBook.

When Jobs resigned in 2011 due to health reasons, Tim Cook, who had served as Chief Operating Officer, took over as CEO. Cook's leadership style marked a significant departure from that of his predecessor. Unlike Jobs, Cook is known for his collaborative approach, emphasizing teamwork, operational efficiency, and an inclusive company culture. Cook focused on leveraging the strengths of his team, encouraging input from all levels of the organization, and fostering a supportive and respectful work environment.

Key Differences in Leadership Styles:

1. **Visionary vs. Collaborative:**
   - **Jobs:** His visionary approach involved setting a clear and bold direction for Apple, often pushing boundaries and challenging norms. His

autocratic style meant he made most of the critical decisions, with little room for dissent.

- **Cook:** Emphasizes collaboration, seeking input from his leadership team and employees. Cook's style is more democratic, encouraging open dialogue and collective decision-making.

2. **Product Focus vs. Operational Excellence:**
   - **Jobs:** Focused intensely on product innovation, design, and user experience. His hands-on involvement in product development was legendary.
   - **Cook:** While still valuing innovation, Cook's strength lies in operational excellence and supply chain management, ensuring Apple's products are delivered efficiently and cost-effectively.
3. **High Standards vs. Inclusivity:**
   - **Jobs:** Known for his perfectionism and demanding nature, Jobs often pushed his team to their limits to achieve exceptional results.
   - **Cook:** Values inclusivity and respect within the workplace, promoting a culture where employees feel valued and supported.

Learning Outcome: This case study demonstrates that different leadership styles can be effective depending on the context and organizational needs. Readers can draw several valuable lessons from this transition:

1.Flexibility in Leadership:

- **Adapting Style:** Effective leaders can adapt their style to fit the organization's evolving needs. Jobs' autocratic style was crucial during Apple's period of intense innovation, while Cook's collaborative approach helped stabilize and grow the company in its mature phase.

- **Context Matters:** The success of a leadership style can depend heavily on the context. Jobs' style worked well for driving breakthrough innovation, whereas Cook's approach has been effective for maintaining operational excellence and long-term sustainability.

2. **Integrating Vision and Collaboration:**
   - **Balanced Approach:** Leaders can benefit from integrating elements of both visionary and collaborative styles. Having a clear vision is essential, but fostering collaboration and inclusivity can help achieve that vision more effectively.
   - **Leveraging Team Strengths:** Encouraging input from team members can lead to better decision-making and a more engaged workforce. Leaders should strive to balance their vision with the collective strengths and insights of their team.
3. **Operational Efficiency and Innovation:**
   - **Dual Focus:** Combining a focus on innovation with strong operational practices can drive sustained success. Leaders should not only aim for groundbreaking ideas but also ensure their efficient implementation.

- **Continuous Improvement:** Maintaining high standards is important, but so is fostering a supportive environment that encourages continuous improvement and employee well-being.

By reflecting on the leadership transition at Apple, readers can gain insights into how to tailor their leadership approach to their specific environment and needs. Whether leading a small team or a large organization, understanding when to employ visionary tactics and when to foster collaboration can significantly enhance leadership effectiveness.

CS 3: 3M's Innovation Culture

Topic: Innovation and Creativity

Description: 3M, a multinational conglomerate known for its wide array of products, has long been a pioneer in fostering a culture of innovation and creativity. One of the cornerstones of this culture is the "15% rule," a policy that allows employees to dedicate up to 15% of their working time to projects of their own choosing. This initiative was established to encourage employees to explore new ideas and pursue personal interests that could potentially benefit the company.

The "15% rule" has been instrumental in driving innovation at 3M, leading to the creation of numerous successful products. One of the most famous examples is the Post-it Note, which emerged from an employee's experimentation with a low-tack adhesive. Initially, the adhesive was deemed a failure because it didn't meet the strong bonding criteria for 3M's main products. However, by having the freedom to explore and persist with the idea, the employee eventually developed a practical application that became one of 3M's most iconic products.

Key Elements of 3M's Innovation Culture:

1. **Encouragement of Autonomy:**
   - **Empowering Employees:** By giving employees the autonomy to work on projects they are passionate about, 3M taps into intrinsic motivation, which is a powerful driver of creativity.
   - **Trust and Freedom:** Employees are trusted to manage their own time and are given the freedom to experiment without the pressure of immediate results.
2. **Structured Support:**
   - **Resources and Tools:** 3M provides the necessary resources and tools for employees to explore their ideas. This includes access to laboratories, materials, and mentorship from more experienced colleagues.
   - **Innovation Programs:** The company has formal programs and networks to support innovation, such as the 3M Tech Forum, which connects scientists and engineers from various disciplines to share ideas and collaborate.
3. **Tolerance for Failure:**
   - **Learning from Mistakes:** 3M understands that not all innovative projects will succeed. By fostering an environment where failure is seen

as a learning opportunity, employees are more willing to take risks and experiment with new concepts.

- **Iterative Process:** The innovation process at 3M is iterative, with continuous refinement and development of ideas based on feedback and trial-and-error.

4. **Recognition and Reward:**
   - **Acknowledging Contributions:** 3M recognizes and rewards innovative contributions, whether they lead to successful products or not. This recognition reinforces the value of creativity and encourages ongoing participation in innovation activities.

Learning Outcome: Readers can draw several valuable lessons from 3M's innovation culture and apply similar strategies to their professional and personal lives:

1. **Implementing Personal Innovation Time:**
   - **Set Aside Time:** Allocate a specific portion of your time, such as a few hours each week, to focus on creative projects or explore new ideas. This dedicated time can lead to breakthroughs and new opportunities.
   - **Encourage Autonomy:** If you are in a leadership position, encourage your team members to dedicate time to personal projects and provide the necessary support and resources.

2. **Creating a Supportive Environment:**
   - **Provide Resources:** Ensure that the necessary tools, materials, and mentorship are available

to support creative endeavors. This includes fostering a collaborative environment where ideas can be freely shared and developed.

- **Build Networks:** Establish formal or informal networks where individuals can connect, share ideas, and collaborate on innovative projects.

3. **Embracing Failure as a Learning Opportunity:**

- **Shift Perspective:** View failures as valuable learning experiences rather than setbacks. Encourage a mindset that sees experimentation and risk-taking as essential components of the innovation process.

- **Iterate and Improve:** Adopt an iterative approach to innovation, continuously refining ideas based on feedback and experience.

4. **Recognizing and Rewarding Creativity:**

- **Acknowledge Efforts:** Recognize and celebrate creative efforts, even if they do not lead to immediate success. This positive reinforcement encourages ongoing innovation and fosters a culture of creativity.

- **Provide Incentives:** Consider implementing incentives or rewards for innovative contributions, such as bonuses, public recognition, or career advancement opportunities.

By adopting these practices, readers can create an environment that nurtures innovation and creativity, both in their professional roles and personal lives. The principles of the "15% rule" can lead to the development of groundbreaking ideas and solutions, driving growth and success in various contexts.

CS 4: Starbucks' Employee Motivation Programs

Topic: Motivation and Engagement

Description: Starbucks has established itself not only as a leading coffee retailer but also as an exemplar of employee motivation and engagement. The company's comprehensive approach to employee benefits, training, and career development opportunities has created a work environment where employees, referred to as "partners," feel valued and invested in the company's success.

Key Elements of Starbucks' Employee Motivation Programs:

1. **Comprehensive Benefits:**
    - **Healthcare and Insurance:** Starbucks offers extensive healthcare benefits to both full-time and part-time employees, covering medical, dental, and vision care. This commitment to employee well-being extends to mental health support and wellness programs.
    - **Stock Options and Financial Rewards:** Through the Bean Stock program, employees are given stock options, allowing them to share in the company's financial success. This financial incentive aligns employees' interests with the company's performance.
    - **Tuition Reimbursement:** Starbucks provides educational support through its College

Achievement Plan, offering full tuition reimbursement for employees who pursue an online bachelor's degree through Arizona State University.

2. **Training and Development:**
   - **Extensive Onboarding:** New hires undergo thorough training that covers not only job-specific skills but also company culture and values. This onboarding process helps employees feel connected to the company from the start.
   - **Ongoing Training Opportunities:** Continuous learning is encouraged through various training programs and workshops. These programs focus on skill development, leadership training, and personal growth.
   - **Mentorship Programs:** Employees have access to mentorship and coaching, fostering professional development and career advancement.
3. **Career Development:**
   - **Clear Career Pathways:** Starbucks provides clear career progression opportunities, encouraging employees to advance within the company. This includes transitioning from barista roles to management positions and beyond.
   - **Leadership Programs:** The company offers leadership training programs designed to develop future leaders within the organization. These programs emphasize the importance of

emotional intelligence, strategic thinking, and effective communication.

4. **Recognition and Appreciation:**
   - **Employee Recognition Programs:** Starbucks has multiple recognition programs to celebrate employee achievements, including the "Partner of the Quarter" and "Green Apron" awards. These initiatives acknowledge hard work and dedication.
   - **Inclusive Culture:** Starbucks promotes an inclusive and supportive work environment where diversity is celebrated, and employees feel respected and valued.

Learning Outcome: By examining Starbucks' approach to employee motivation and engagement, readers can glean several actionable strategies to enhance motivation in their own professional and personal lives:

1. **Offering Comprehensive Benefits:**
   - **Healthcare and Well-being:** Prioritize employee well-being by offering comprehensive health benefits and wellness programs. For personal application, individuals can ensure they maintain a healthy work-life balance and seek employers who value their well-being.
   - **Financial Incentives:** Implement financial rewards such as profit-sharing or stock options to align employees' interests with the organization's success. Personally, setting financial goals and celebrating milestones can boost motivation.

2. **Providing Training and Development Opportunities:**

    - **Continuous Learning:** Foster a culture of continuous learning by offering ongoing training and development opportunities. Encourage employees to pursue new skills and career growth.

    - **Mentorship and Coaching:** Establish mentorship programs to support professional development. Individuals can seek mentors or become mentors to foster growth and share knowledge.

3. **Creating Clear Career Development Pathways:**

    - **Career Progression:** Develop clear career pathways within the organization to encourage employees to envision their future with the company. Personally, setting clear career goals and pursuing professional development can drive motivation.

    - **Leadership Development:** Invest in leadership training programs to develop future leaders. Individuals can seek leadership training and opportunities to enhance their leadership skills.

4. **Recognition and Appreciation:**

    - **Employee Recognition:** Implement regular recognition programs to celebrate employee achievements and contributions. Personally, acknowledging and celebrating personal achievements can boost motivation.

- **Inclusive Culture:** Promote an inclusive and supportive work environment where diversity is celebrated. Individuals can contribute to creating an inclusive atmosphere by respecting and valuing diverse perspectives.

By adopting these motivational techniques from Starbucks, readers can enhance engagement and motivation within their teams and organizations, as well as in their personal pursuits. Recognizing and valuing employees' contributions, providing opportunities for growth, and fostering a supportive environment are key strategies for sustaining motivation and achieving success.

Appendix B: Interactive Exercises for Developing a Strong Organizational Culture

Part I: Foundations of Management Psychology

Activity 1: Behavioral Observation Exercise

- **Objective:** Understand human behavior in the workplace.
- **Instructions:** Spend a day observing a team within your organization. Take notes on different behaviors exhibited by team members, focusing on communication styles, decision-making processes, and conflict resolution methods. Reflect on how these behaviors impact team dynamics and overall productivity.

Activity 2: Personality Assessment Workshop

- **Objective:** Explore the impact of personality traits on management.
- **Instructions:** Administer a widely recognized personality assessment (e.g., Myers-Briggs Type Indicator) to your team. Discuss the results in a group setting, highlighting how different personality traits can be leveraged for effective management and improved team collaboration.

Part II: Psychological Approaches to Management

Activity 3: Decision-Making Simulation

- **Objective:** Enhance cognitive processes in decision-making.
- **Instructions:** Create a simulation involving a complex business decision that requires input from multiple team members. Divide participants into small groups and assign roles. After the simulation, discuss the cognitive processes used and evaluate the effectiveness of the decisions made.

Activity 4: Leadership Style Analysis

- **Objective:** Understand different leadership psychology approaches.
- **Instructions:** Present case studies of various leadership styles (e.g., transformational, transactional, servant leadership). Have participants analyze each case and discuss the psychological principles underpinning each style, as well as their effectiveness in different organizational contexts.

Activity 5: Motivation and Engagement Survey

- **Objective:** Assess and improve motivation and engagement.
- **Instructions:** Develop a survey to measure current levels of motivation and engagement within your team. Analyze the results and create an action plan to address any areas of concern, utilizing motivational theories and techniques discussed in the book.

Part III: Organizational Behavior and Culture

Activity 6: Communication Skills Workshop

- **Objective:** Improve communication and interpersonal relations.
- **Instructions:** Conduct a workshop focused on active listening, non-verbal communication, and conflict resolution. Use role-playing scenarios to practice and reinforce these skills, followed by group discussions on how effective communication enhances organizational culture.

Activity 7: Team Building Challenge

- **Objective:** Strengthen team dynamics.
- **Instructions:** Organize a team-building activity, such as an escape room or a problem-solving challenge. After completing the activity, hold a debrief session to discuss how team dynamics influenced the outcome and how these insights can be applied to improve teamwork in the workplace.

Activity 8: Cultural Assessment and Action Plan

- **Objective:** Evaluate and enhance organizational structure and culture.
- **Instructions:** Conduct an organizational culture assessment using surveys or interviews. Analyze the findings and develop a comprehensive action plan to strengthen positive cultural attributes and address any weaknesses identified.

Part IV: Applying Psychology to Management Practices

Activity 9: Performance Management Review

- **Objective:** Implement effective performance management techniques.
- **Instructions:** Review and analyze your current performance management system. Identify areas for improvement and redesign the system using psychological principles to ensure it motivates and develops employees effectively.

Activity 10: Stress Management Workshop

- **Objective:** Promote well-being and coping mechanisms.
- **Instructions:** Organize a workshop on stress management techniques, such as mindfulness, time management, and relaxation exercises. Encourage participants to share their experiences and create personalized stress management plans.

Activity 11: Innovation and Creativity Brainstorming Session

- **Objective:** Foster a culture of innovation.
- **Instructions:** Hold a brainstorming session focused on generating innovative ideas to solve a specific organizational challenge. Use creative thinking techniques, such as mind mapping and lateral thinking, to encourage diverse perspectives and solutions.

Activity 12: Future Trends Discussion Panel

- **Objective:** Prepare for future trends and challenges.

- **Instructions:** Host a panel discussion with experts on remote and hybrid work models and the use of technology in management. Encourage participants to ask questions and discuss how these trends will impact their organization, and develop strategies to adapt to these changes.